HERB MARTINEZ'S GUIDE TO
Pinstriping

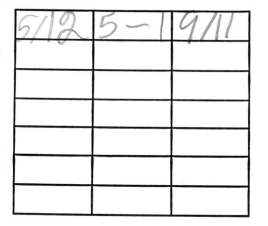

Herb Martinez

©2006 Herb Martinez
Published by

krause publications
An Imprint of F+W Publications

700 East State Street • Iola, WI 54990-0001
715-445-2214 • 888-457-2873
www.krausebooks.com

Our toll-free number to place an order or obtain
a free catalog is (800) 258-0929.

Library of Congress Catalog Number: 2006938534
ISBN 13: 978-0-89689-244-6
ISBN 10: 0-89689-244-1

Designed by Paul Birling
Edited by Brian Earnest

Printed in United States of America

Dedication & Acknowledgments

The subject of pinstriping and its associated arts has been covered many times in many ways, from short articles in automotive magazines, to lengthy chapters in books published for the industry. Most of these articles pertain to sign painting, custom painting and airbrushing. The subject of pinstriping has never been covered in the way is try to present it to you in these pages. I have dedicated most of my life to the pursuit of the perfection of the line and design. My intention in these pages is to show you the techniques, with examples of how to do it yourself, that have made my chosen profession a success for me.

Without a mentor, it's very difficult to learn anything. You need someone to, at the very least, take the time to let you hang around their shop and observe techniques for laying lines and designs. My first mentor, Tommy "The Greek" Hrones offered me the opportunity to come into his shop and watch the work being done. Without this influence, I probably would never have given pinstriping more than a passing interest. Also,

without coach or teacher, it's nearly impossible to make any headway in learning the art of pinstriping. "Saint John" Morton was that coach for me and I still look to him for advice from time to time. He's even been beneficial in helping me write this book. It was his teaching and patience that gave me the confidence to keep going and learn both striping and custom paint in the early 1960s. At that time no one was sharing any information or ideas within the industry. John took an interest in me, however, and he shared his talent for the line and design.

Just as important, without getting some sort of break, it's very difficult to succeed as a full-time striper. Cary Greenwood gave me that break early in my career. Without Cary I would probably still be in the bodyshops painting cars.

This book is dedicated is to those men who helped me, and all the other artists that showed me a little trick here and a little trick there. All these people, in one way or another, helped me to experience what it is to pick up a brush and do wonderful things with it.

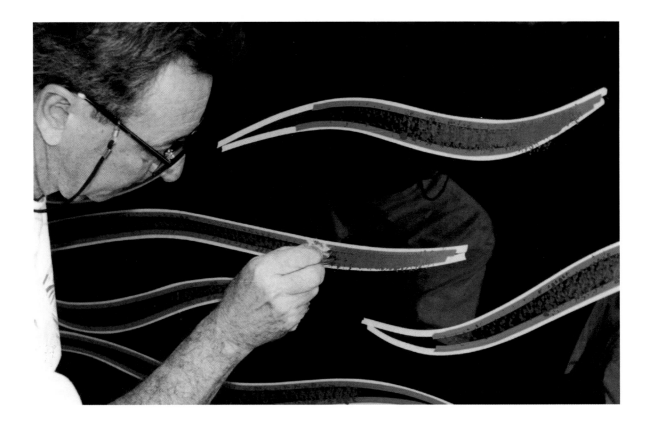

I would also like to recognize Doc Guthrey and Richard Shelton from Los Angeles Trade Technical College, Steve Fineberg, who taught me curly Q's, and Al Meadows, who inspired me to do signs and really be an artist, not just a pinstriper. To Von Dutch, who pointed out that you have to have artistic talent to do pinstriping (before that revelation I thought just about anyone could do it). Ed Roth, who helped me watch my marketing, and Eddie Paul, who showed me how to truly do it in the style George Barris used on the cars in the magazines. Believe me, there is nothing like one-on-one training. And last, but certainly not least, to all the stripers I have shared shops and easels with during Panel Jams. Thanks for all I learned from you, and man that's a lot.

You might not have any intentions of becoming a professional or operating a shop. Just let me give you this piece of advice: the art itself will tell you what to do. No matter what kind of medium or style of art you may chose, if you listen to your heart, your imagination will follow. I have seen artists in many mediums — oils, gels and watercolors to mention just a few — that just can't help themselves. They create and create and create; it's their passion. Once you learn the basics, striping will probably be the same way; art is art. Just go with the flow and create to your heart's content. As you create, you will be practicing the lines that may very well make you money someday. Early in my career I acquired a yearning for doing business as it relates to the art and I haven't quite been the same since. This is my passion, just as you will find yours, so get going. You only have 2 million more miles of striping lines to go before you'll start to think you're good at this art.

Good luck to you all, and always remember to "keep it wet."

Table Of Contents

Foreword

By Eddie Paul

I n my 37 years of designing and building movie cars for major motion pictures, as well as the automotive industry, I have come across a very diverse group of people. A few of them you want to forget shortly after meeting them, but most you want to remember. In that latter group is an even smaller group which you form a lifetime bond with and proudly call your friends. Herb Martinez is in this group. In the 35-plus years that I have known Herb he has not changed a bit, nor has he ever strayed from his goal of becoming one of, if not the best, pinstripers in the world.

When Herb asked me to write the Foreword for his book, I was flattered and excited to blow Herb's horn for him. But, I must confess that I had a problem writing this Foreword. After making a brief outline of Herb's high points, I was worried there was no room left for the book. It is difficult to limit my superlatives and stick to simple praise of Herb's talents.

It's true that you do need more than just talent in this world, especially if you are self employed, as Herb is, so he has spent a lot of time on business skills as well as people skills, which are worthless if not backed by honesty and dependability.

If Herb says something will happen, it will. On this you can rely. So, I was not the least bit apprehensive to recommend Herb to Krause Publications, even though I knew Herb had never written a book before.

Beyond that, as far as I am concerned, Herb is the world's best pinstriper. It may just take the rest of the world time to figure this out.

I have sometimes been accused of being before my time, and picking winners to a race yet to take place, so hang in there Herb your day is just around the corner. This book will set you apart from the large group of talkers, and puts you in an elite group of the doers!

Move over Von Dutch, Tommy the Greek and Ed Roth and make room for Herb Martinez!

— Eddie Paul

Introduction

This book is for the sole purpose of making sure that all the small articles ever written on the subject of pinstriping got put together and told in their entirety and not abbreviated. Nothing frustrates a person trying to learn something more than getting half the story or half the picture. In this book I intend to pursue any means possible to teach you, the reader, all the tricks, tips, and just plain common knowledge about the techniques and the art of pinstriping.

The booklet pictured is Eddie Paul's first attempt at writing a "how-to" from 1979. Considering the lack of space and the economy of words used to explain a very complicated subject, he did very well. Later, Eddie put together the first "How to Pinstripe" video using yours truly as the model. That was 1983. It was revised from 1/2-inch format to 3/4-inch professional format in 1984. In 2002 we teamed up again to do a much-needed update in CircleScan 4D. In 2004, Eddie added 10 more minutes on to the video and The Eastwood Company now distributes it.

Since then, I have thought a lot about what I could write in book form about the art that has now become my

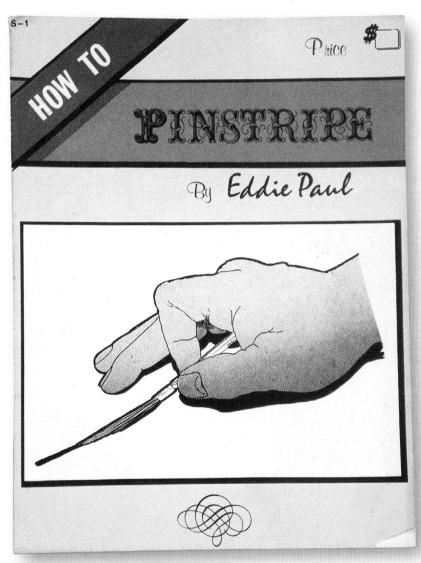

life's work. Most guys have the good sense to go find something they can make good money at. I never got the memo! Oh well. I'm very happy doing what I've done with my life. It's been a great experience to show people how to do what I do. I thought my publisher was crazy when I was asked to write a book on this subject. It could be explained so much better in video format. Well, time will tell if I'm right or not. I have had many years since that first video to think of ways to explain everything about pinstriping in ways that the average person could understand. My propensity to use slang words, however, has always held me up. This why I have also included a glossary of terms and

words in this book, so you can translate my sometimes non-comprehensible thoughts.

We will go through history, techniques, theories, and the business aspects of pinstriping. There is a lot to be said and I thank my publishers for giving me the opportunity and the space to get all of it down on paper. Not all of the text is my work. You can't realistically explain pinstriping without getting a number of opinions and ideas. I've called on the best of the best to help me write this book. That's a lot of experts putting a lot of experience and information out there for you. I hope you enjoy the book, and like a striper friend of mine says, "keep it wet."

Chapter One

In The Beginning, There Was Line Art

Throughout history we have seen the progress of art, be it lines or designs or characters or murals. Cave dwellers did it, Egyptians did it, Romans and Greeks. Everybody had lines. Henney Youngman had lines: "take my wife…please."

The roots of original line art can be traced back to the cave drawings in the La Grotte Chauvet-Pont-d"Arc in France. This sudden emergence of line art is among the most significan inventions of the Aurignacian culture, occupying the vast geographic area from the High-Danube area of Germany, through Austria, the Monrovianm region of Slovakia, and in the Santander region of Spain. In France, the Aurignacian people inhabited small valleys and piedmonts of the Pyrean mountains. Among the

This Egyptian coffin from the collection of the British Museum shows the same type of decorations used on the Roman and Greek chariots.

significant innovations of the Aurignacians was the development of body ornamentation, including pierced shells and teeth, carved bone pendants, bracelets, and ivory beads. This art dates back 31,000 years.

A Brief Twisted History of Pinstriping and The Art of the Line

By Andy Leipzig

Many people assume that pinstriping is associated with hot rod giants such as Von Dutch, George Barris and a host of others. Actually, its origins can be traced all the way back the earliest French cave paintings. These amazingly elegant and simple line gestures point to symbolism that related to the painters' culture perhaps more than some religious practices. American Indians, whose line work demonstrated a whole new depth and spirituality, used pictograms, vibrant colors, and freestyle gestures to capture the spirit of their surroundings.

From caves to teepees to remote tropical islands in the Pacific, the art of the line has a constant thread: It has been a form of expression that has unified cultures and expressed individuality throughout human history. On the South Pacific islands of Tahiti and Moorea, unique style was not only found in tribal tattoos, but also in decorative carvings.

A good example of fire wagons of the turn of the century is this example from the Oakland, California, Museum. It was decorated by celebrated artisan/ sign painter Neils Hoegsberg, formally from Denmark.

By the end of the 19th century, trade shows, county fairs, and world fairs had displays of machinery of all types, decorated with striping, gold leafing and signage that would wow the crowds and attract attention to the product.

Early Roman Greek and Etruscan works, particularly black and white urns, depict athletes and lifestyles through line work. This type of artwork was also included in their architecture and geometric patterning, flags, and their chariots.

It's far easier to trace the beginnings of metallurgy and twisting metal than it is to track the origins of a line gesture. Throughout our history, though, it is certain that almost as soon as an item was crafted through trials of fire, it was ornamented.

The art of freehand pinstriping has been in existence for many years. Painted stripes have appeared on every antique imaginable. Pianos, furniture, sculptures, vases, picture frames, wagons — the list is endless. Tune in to this art and you will find it evidenced in places you'd never suspect.

Many writers have told stories and drawn pictures of how Roman and Greek chariots were decorated. The only evidence I was able to photograph was that of a coffin in the Egyptian collection in the British Museum in London. It shows the same type of decoration I have heard described on the chariots from the golden age. Coaches and wagons in later times were decorated with various forms of filigree and coats of arms or signage. By the end of the 19th century, trade shows, county fairs, and world fairs had displays of machinery of all types, decorated with striping, gold leafing, and signage that wowed crowds and attracted attention to the product.

These are two very fine examples of turn-of-the-century auto/carriage decoration. The vehicles are from the Bugatti-Schlumph Museum in Lyon, France.

Striping In The New Century

By 1900, the automobile had been invented and we were well on our way to replacing the carriage and buggy with the horseless carriage. Builders were not only pinstriping autos, but buses in London, runabouts in France, and course, fire wagons and later trucks in the U.S.

Many painters took up striping over the next 30 years, and most worked in wagon factories. Men who cut their teeth on wooden vehicles were soon working assembly lines. Henry Ford is rumored to have paid his stripers a dollar more a day to stripe than other workers.

These two Model A Fords feature the original pinstriping done on the assembly line. Both cars are from the J.W. Silvera collection.

By the late 1940s, sprint and midget race cars began to be adorned with more than just numbers and scallops. These fine examples were displayed at the 1949 and 1950 Grand National Roadster Show. The numbers were outlined, as were the scallops. The Romeo "Dago" Palamides car (top) was teardrop pinstriped as well. This was a turning point for pinstriping. It happened initially mostly in northern California.

By the late 1940s sprint midget racecars and track roadsters had all the trimmings, including pinstriped outlines on the scallops and decorative accents all around the car. This trend was mostly seen in the northern California area with Tommy the Greek leading the way in design. The Bay Area track roadsters were particularly noted for their chrome, trick paint and upholstery. Pat Granahl, in his new book on Von Dutch, credits this phenomenon to the first official

Grand National Roaster Show's initial entrants. This "impromptu gathering," as he calls it, led to *Hot Rod Magazine* following up with the winners of the show featured in the magazine, but the stripers were not mentioned. However, if you look at the style of scallops and pinstriping, you can recognize the style Tommy the Greek. Von Dutch later stated in a letter that Tommy was one of his primary influences. Also noteworthy was the absence of any striping on the cars coming from southern California.

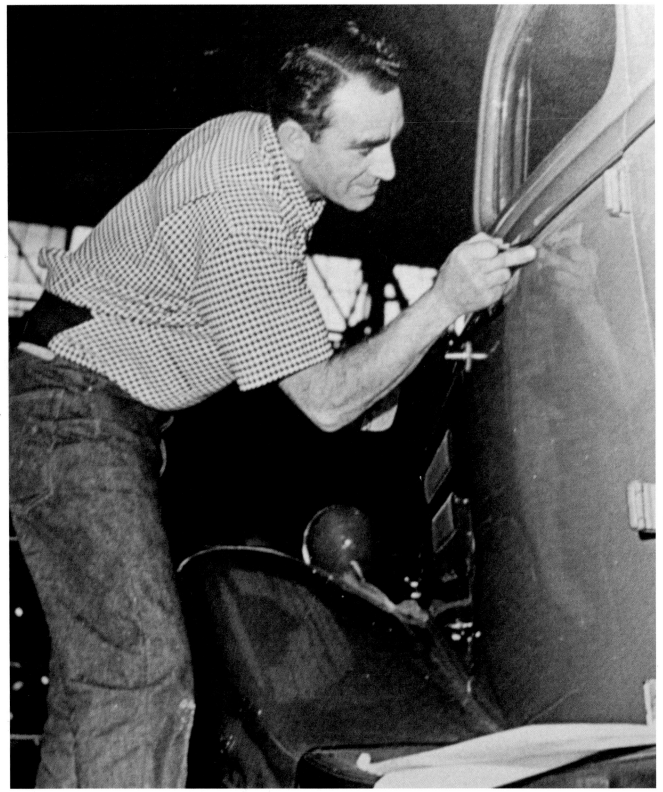

Tommy "The Greek" Hrones was the leader of the pack. By 1950 he had started to change the amount of striping on our cars. He is famous for his scallops and "teardrop" designs. Even Von Dutch was influenced significantly by The Greek.

Assembly line stripers began making their way from the plants to the shops, with most of them changing jobs just to keep their family's fed. Pinstriping still had a few years to go before it becomes the "modern line" and the newest trend to hit L.A. Later, the magazines like *Hot Rod*, *Rod & Custom*, *Car Craft* and others spread the pinstriping trend all over the country. By the mid- and late-'50s, pinstripers could work and have a good backlog for weeks to come. Pinstriping was about to hit its heyday.

The Modern Line Begins

Some of the early "modern" pinstripers were true entrepreneurs and realized quickly that a good way to generate spending money was to stripe a buddy's car for a little extra money. Most early stripers were probably on a similar track, but more than likely were doing it to just to stay alive, rather than get ahead.

Von Dutch described it best in his interview with Ed "Big Daddy" Roth sometime in the late 1980s. He said that he saw guys that would go to used car lots and stripe cars for just a few bucks. Dutch picked up the idea and ran with it. A few other guys followed suit and did the same thing. Perhaps the motivations of these men were different, but the outcome was the same, and the early version of the trade was born. Some of these guys started the pinstriping craze of the 1950s, while others simply added to it.

Pinstriping grew in popularity because of the mass exposure of Von Dutch (who hated it all), and through the increasing number of pinstripe jobs out there on the streets and in the shows. Pinstriping made its initial appearance on dashboards and then made its way outside to the hoods and deck lids of custom cars and hot rods. In 1954, you rarely saw pinstriping on a car. By 1958, it was all over the car. The trend blanketed the hot rod and custom world, and Los Angeles was ground zero. Magazines east and west covered the trend like it was manna from heaven. Dutch was our hero. He appeared in numerous publications. Even a teen-oriented magazine called *Dig*.

Dutch believed modern pinstriping started at a body shop when one of his customers asked him if he could cover up some grinder marks created when a hood and

The pinstriping trend of the 1950s was covered by all the car magazines of the day.

deck lid were shaved off and molded. This occurred often when the final paint was applied and the primer shrunk back down, leaving grinder marks. He said he covered the first grinder mark with a line shaped exactly like the mark itself and then followed suit with another to match it on the other side in mirror image. Then another mark was covered and another line was mirrored and so on, until he had created a design.

In researching this book, we put out a questionnaire to a number of former and current stripers. These are craftsmen who have been in the trade since the 1940s and '50s and still remember what it was like to be a budding artist with a brush back in the days of the beginning of the modern line.

Andy Southard Jr. learned striping from Dean Jefferies and photography from the New York Institute of Photography. He went on to be one of the best in both fields. He wrote the book on many of the customs and hot rods and the Grand National Roadster Show.

"Saint John" Morton
Age 64
Current resident of Aptos CA
50 years experience in pinstriping, custom paint, and paint manufacturing. He's a Bay Area boy, born and bred.

Larry Watson
Age 66
Current resident of Victorville, CA
One of the legends of custom paint, but he started by pinstriping cars for $5 each at the age of 17.

Mike Clines
Current resident of Sacramento, CA
52 years experience in pinstriping. Mike is the guy that striped for Larry Watson when Larry got too busy painting.

Tom Kelly
(ageless)
Current business residence is Bellflower, CA
52 years experience in pinstriping and signs. In the dictionary, if you look up fast, Kelly's picture is there. He was the grandson of the famous "Baron" of the Crazy Painters team back in the 1950s. The other member was Ed "Big Daddy" Roth.

Bobbo Dunn
Age 73
Currently residing in Albuquerque, NM
60 years experience in pinstriping, custom paint, airbrush, and loads of other stuff. In the 1950 he he was considered the "Von Dutch of Pomona, CA".

Nat Quick
Age 62
Currently residing in Petaluma, CA
47 years experience in pinstriping, custom paint, airbrush, and now fine art. Nat's claim to fame is he is the "father" of headlights and taillights airbrushed on funny cars. He and Kenny Youngblood were a team at Kirby's back in the day. Best fat line guy I ever saw stripe.

Don "the Egyptian" Boeke
Age 65
Currently residing in Dayton, OH
48 years experience in pinstriping, custom paint, airbrush, and auto body. In the Midwest, everyone has heard of Don. A true legend of the trade.

Jon Kosmoski
Age 66
Currently residing in Minneapolis, MN
50 years experience in pinstriping, spray painting, and paint manufacturing. His House of Kolor line of custom paints is the standard of the industry today.

"East Coast Artie" Schilling
Age 60
Currently residing in Surfside Beach, N.C.
47 years experience pinstriping and signs. He saw it all while working in New York.

Andy Southard Jr.
Age 72
Currently residing in Monterey, CA.
Forty experience striping, Andy is also one of the major names in the automotive publishing business. His articles and books have been seen and read for 40 years. He has recently published books on customs, hot rods and car shows.

This happy bunch fellows gathered for the first Pinheads Speed Striping Nationals at Lead East, New Jersey, in 1993.

This 1940 Ford was the "Original Pinheads Pace Car" and our official mascot.

All of these guys answered the call of pinstriping in the 1950s. Not all were artistic about it at first. Some guys just did lines on used cars, which were the antique cars of today — 1920s and 30s roadsters, coupes and sedans. Most stripers saw lines in a magazines or at a car show and learned on their own or through a mentor. Artie Schilling had "Kenny the Striper" teach him, while Andy Southard had Dean Jeffries show him a thing or two. The going price back then was $3 to $10 a car. That was a lot of money for a kid at the time.

Most painters started in their local areas where they grew up. Grumbacher, Mack, so-called "German's", and Hamilton's or Handovers were the choice of brush. The paint choice was either Sherwin Williams, 1 Shot, or Ronan enamels, or Veco striping lacquer. The survivors today are 1 Shot enamel and House of Kolor urethane enamel. Ronan is still making a line of striping paint.

The names of mentors varied with the area of the country, but a few stripers names kept popping up. Von Dutch was a huge influence as was Tommy the Greek from Oakland. In the latest book from Pat Granahl, Tommy is mentioned as a huge influence on Von Dutch. Los Angeles always had great stripers, like Art Summers and "The Baron." Baron was one of the stripers at the Studebaker wagon works and later a striper for Ford on the assembly line for 25 years.

Later it was Dean Jeffries and Larry Watson. In the Midwest, Don Boeke and Jon Kosmoski were watching Dutch and Tommy also, but got further influence from

The right rear fender of the Pinheads Pace Car is one of many body panels on the car done in various styles by many different stripers from all over the world.

Cliff Anderson Jr., Dave Eckel, and Jim Norris. In the east, along with Kenny the Mad Striper, there was Johnny Palone at the House of Pinstripes, Vic Kesler from Queens, New York, Don Ives, Nicky Rorro, and Vinnie the Pinstriper from New York City.

Most all these guys went on to other types of work, from painting signs and cars to making the paint itself. Jeffries got into building and painting cars for the movie and TV industries, while Larry Watson got into acting while keeping his "day job" painting cars. Some are now retired or semi-retired. Nat Quick is now doing fine art canvases of World War II planes. Most all of them still stripe from time to time, if not everyday.

A lot of the decoration of today's cars is being done by computer, tape and machines. But, with all this happening, the interest in hand-painted "automotive abstract art" is very high. There are more books, videos, and workshops being done on the subjects of auto art than ever before. "Old school" styles have gained tremendous popularity. The so-called "rat rod" has really made a difference in the amount of old school striping designs being done. TV has also played a huge

role in getting young people interested in the trade. And thanks to all the great stripers of the past, the bar has been set very high for quality. We're not poking around in the dark anymore, as in the 1950s.

So where are we going in this world of stickers and striping machines all trying to share the striping spotlight? The truth is that striping really hasn't changed all that much in all these years. The last few years some new-breed guys like Craig Frasher have contributed to a new look of outlining flames with what he calls "slash striping." The line is skewed and looks very rough. Craig started this style when he couldn't get a striper to come and outline a flame job that had to be finished for an upcoming car show. Craig took matters into his own hands and picked up a brush that he had no experience with and proceeded to stripe the flame outline in this "slash" manner. It got rave reviews and the style went on to be another trend, invented out of necessity, just like Von Dutch, when he invented the modern pinstriping designs to cover up grinder marks. With the advent of all the automotive reality and information shows, the demand for striping and numbers of people interested in learning to stripe has grown tremendously.

Chapter Two

The Tools of the Trade

I n the world of pinstriping and airbrush art, our tools are second in importance only to our talents to use them. These tools of our trade can be as common as a 12-inch ruler, or as scarce as some out-of-manufacture specialty brushes.

Wax and Grease Removers

I have a rule about cleaning a car: If it won't come clean with either solvent or something like water (sometimes a little spit works well), you have a problem. My favorite cleaner is R-M Pre-Kleano (#900) and DuPont #3864 "Vari-Temp" in a 50/50 combination. Pre-Kleano is a solvent-borne cleaner designed to remove silicone, wax, grease, road tar and oils from painted surfaces or fiberglass resins. Vari-Temp is a medium-temperature automotive enamel reducer. It has a chemical called

Toluene in it that is extremely carcinogenic. However, it has the ability to turn polymer wax into dust on contact. I was told about this combination of solvents in the early 1980s by Chuck "Shaky Jake" Babbitt of Newport Beach, California. He used it for busting polymer waxes and Cosmolene used in prepping Volkswagens and Porsche's for shipment to America. Shakey swore by this stuff and so do I, providing you clean the surface correctly. I'll explain that later.

Most companies that manufacture paints have a line of solvents for cleaning the surface. There are companies that also make water-based cleaners. Rapid Prep is a non-hazardous wash solvent that removes wax and grease almost like regular solvent-based removers. It's non-flammable, water-based, and non-toxic. Poly Cracker is another water-borne solution. It was invented for the sole purpose of eliminating polymer wax, Armor-All, and mold release agents. But overall, these water borne solvents and cleaners, unfortunately, just don't do the job as well as regular flammable, hazardous and toxic solvents.

You can also eliminate waxes, etc. with denaturized alcohol — otherwise know, as shellac thinner. For eliminating static electricity, use isopropyl alcohol (rubbing alcohol) or water. It will kill the static instantly. This includes the static that builds from those pesky PT Cruiser burst panels that look like glove box doors in the early model years to 2004.

Whatever you use, make sure that you have a good clean surface on which to apply your paint. Surface prep means everything to the longevity of your work.

Shop Towels-Rags-Paper Towels

After you've spent a little money getting the right cleaning solution, you might want to spend a little more and use the proper tool to apply and remove the cleaner off the surface. The common tool is the always-popular "rag," otherwise known as a "shop towel." If possible, use white ones. They have been cleaned special to remove any silicone that could contaminate the surface. My advice is to buy them in packs of 100 from a warehouse outlet like Costco or Sam's Club.

These type of places also sell real cotton terry towels. These are what I use for surface prep. They're soft enough to use on most surfaces and don't leave scratches — fine or otherwise. Paper towels will leave scratches. This

is why optometrists tell you not to use paper towels when cleaning your glasses. If paper will scratch glass or plastic, it will surely scratch a painted surface.

Here's a little tip used by guys like Ed "Big Daddy" Roth and others when they clean the surface of something: If you want to put a little "tooth" on the surface, put a little Comet or Ajax cleaning powder on the rag. Do this with the rag wet with wax and grease remover. This powder will add some fine scratching to the surface and make it easier for the paint to adhere to the surface. I use this trick any time I'm prepping a boat for lettering or striping.

Cotton terry towels are great for cleaning and removing wax and grease remover, but here's another tip: First wash all the rags while they are brand new in your washing machine in hot water and soap. Line dry or machine dry them, but don't use any fabric softener. Softener contains silicone. That's the very stuff you're trying to eliminate.

You can also clean the surface after using the solvent with glass cleaner. If there is any "haze" from the residue if the solvent, the glass cleaner will remove it.

Last, but not least, when using any solvent that's toxic, always wear a proper glove on the hand you're using to apply it. The neoprene gloves I use are available at most

There are many masking tapes available. Some are paper-backed, while others are plastic. Some are common, such as Scotch Tape; others are found only overseas in metric sizes.

hardware stores. Stanley and other companies make them. There are very thick and not good for picking up pennies or anything else small, but use them. I lost a very good friend and a magnificent striper named Chuck "Shakey Jake" Babbit to three different types of cancer, one bout after the other, that may well have been caused by the carcinogens in the remover. This stuff is very dangerous. Please, use that glove.

Tapes and Masks

There is a large variety of tape available, and most of it is from 3M. I trust these guys. I have been using their products my entire career. Their products are not the cheapest out there, but I have always said "penny wise and pound foolish" is no way to be. Some tapes seem expensive, but you have to ask the question, "How much money am I spending for this expense, and how much money will I make (or save) from the job?" Most times the expense is a very small percentage of the final profit.

"Paper or Plastic?"

It's important to use the right tape and use it correctly. Most paper tapes, such as the ones found in hardware and home stores, are OK for masking but very bad for masking edges to block off paint. Regular masking tapes (3M Series 233 Automotive Refinish) will allow the paint to seep under the tape edge, thus causing a "bleed through."

I use a lot of 1/4-inch tape for my layouts, both straight and curvy. But even the curvy layouts have a different result if you use the wrong-size tape. For instance, I use 1/4-inch tape for my flame layouts that are medium to large, and 1/8-inch tape for tighter areas such as motorcycle tanks, fenders, and associated parts like saddlebags and side covers. If you don't plan to have the paint touch the edge of the tape, then this is the product application for you.

However, there is a way, to avoid any paint bleed through. By using the newer, lime green color masking tapes (233+ Performance Masking Tape) you can lay down the tape and use your fingernail as a squeegee to press down the tape, thus forming a barrier. The glue backing in the newer tape is a little more aggressive

than the older beige color tape. By "mashing" the edge down hard you can get the tape to do the job that most plastic tapes are made to do. By the way, at the time of this writing, 3M plans to discontinue making the beige-colored tape for automotive use. In that case, the only tape that will be available will be the lime-colored tape. It is available in sizes from 1/8 inch up to 2 inches in the U.S., and in varying sizes in Europe and Asia.

After researching the Japanese and European markets for the same products, I quickly found out that what exists here does not exist in the same form oveseas. Tapes are found under different part number sand obviously different size. All this information is available on 3M's Web site. Just pick a country and go. In Asia and Europe they use the metric system. For example, 1/4-inch tape is the same as 6 millimeter, and so on for different sizes. 3M makes five different applications of tape for Germany. England has another group of tapes. I didn't see my favorite-size tape (1/4-inch or 6 millimeter) mentioned in the sizes available. I have seen a 3M product in Japan and Germany that's golden yellow in color and 6 millimeters wide by 18 meters long. It's this little tiny thing that defies description. I thought that I had seen it all until I saw this tape. The striper from Mooneyes Japan, "Wildman" Ishi, had stacks of this stuff for the "Pinstriping College" he teaches at the Yokohama Rod & Custom Show each year in December.

Plastic or vinyl tape is used for masking designs and graphics. It comes in a green that is used for straight and slightly curved masking, and a blue tape that is much more flexible for masking graphics, flames, or any application needing a complete block-off of paint on the edges. There is nothing out there that I know of that matches the performance of this tape.

Another brand to consider is Finesse striping tapes. The "Edge" fine line masking tape is OK, but it tends to "pucker up" at the edge on the inside of tight corners. Finesse also has a stencil tape called the "Striper" that comes in varying widths..

Last but not least is 3M's Magic Tape. Sound familiar? It's because you can buy it most anywhere "Scotch Tape" is sold. For the money, it's the cheapest and best way to block off a line or use for a top or base line foe a stripe or letter. The paint doesn't get under the tape and leaves a really clean line. There are varying sizes of this tape, but it's only available at places like sign supply companies or drafting supply stores. It's usually 1/4-inch wide.

House of Kolor Paints & Lacquers

When I first started striping in 1959, I was using a paint product that felt like House of Kolor Urethane Striping Enamel. What do I mean by "feel"? Well, it's that slight "drag" or friction that comes from using a lacquer or urethane striping paint. Back in the old days of striping on the assembly lines, you had to use striping lacquer in order to get the job done faster and get it to dry quickly. You didn't want to mess up a striping job on an assembly line or you could loose your job.

Several companies made striping lacquer in the late 1930s. At that time it was the way to go. Over the years factory striping dwindled and by 1946, when automobile resumed after World War II, there were only a few cars that had any striping at all. DuPont and Veco were the last companies to make striping lacquers available. By the late 1950s they were discontinued.

So what is striping lacquer? Veco Striping Color, as it was called, was a compound of varnish and nitro-cellulous lacquer pigments. It would dry fairly fast but still could be wiped off the same way we wipe off enamels. When I first started watching Tommy the Greek in 1959, he was using Veco. He would screw up a line just to watch the owner of the car react to the mistake. Tommy would always wipe it off and do it right.

In the early to mid 1970s, Paul Morra of Hayward, California, started producing DagerLac in response to the amount of work he was doing for Arlen Ness on motorcycles. It would dry fast and he could clear over it in acrylic lacquer. You couldn't do that then with 1 Shot or the enamel would "lift," or wrinkle. Today, the DagerLac brand is called MoLac and is owned by Seelig Supply in Los Angeles. It is still sold to all the "old school" guys who want to use lacquer instead of urethane.

Some people get nervous because the urethane enamels last better with the addition of a catalyst. These catalysts or hardeners are made for all types of striping paint, enamel or urethanes and contain a very carcinogenic ingredient called Isocyantes. Anytime I'm using this stuff in my color I'm either "gloved up"

These are all the House Of Kolor products for pinstriping: paint, thinner and catalyst. They even have a silicone inhibitor.

or not touching the paint at all. If I get any on me, I immediately clean it off. So what's the advantage of using House of Kolor Urethane Striping Enamel? Drying speed. You can go over your work with your hand or another color within 10 to 20 minutes of application instead of having to wait 2 to 12 hours for your first color to dry.

Practice using these urethanes before applying them to real job. If you make a mistake, it could cost you a brand new paint job. This is especially true with lacquers.

The best rule of thumb is to follow, word for word, the directions for using this product directly from House of Kolor's manuals. And remember, mixing paint with no respirator can be very dangerous to your health.

This product is a striping and lettering enamel. It is designed solely for the purpose of striping, lettering and airbrush work. It has high pigmentation, but low solids in order to keep a minimal edge and a more "open" coat time for longer drying. "Solid" refers to the resin-to-solvent ratio. High solids = 70 percent resin, 30 percent solvent. The 70 percent = high solids is only hypothetical. Paint companies use different ratios (45 percent, 50 percent, etc. You can top coat the paint with lacquers, urethane enamel, acrylic enamel or alkyd enamel.

The striping paint can be applied in several ways. You can pre-mix the color or mix and apply as you go. HOK recommends depositing one to two loads of color onto the palette and dipping your brush occasionally in a shot glass of thinner to give it brushing consistency. Some stripers will actually mix their hardener right into the thinner. It takes that extra step of mixing hardener in the paint out of the equation.

Pre-mixing is easier for me. I like being able to go right to the paint and not have to worry about putting in thinner or hardener in the mix while I'm paletting my brush. You will, however, need to occasionally dip your brush in thinner and work it around to thin the drying paint in your brush. I use the paint and hardener combination without any thinner mixed in the paint at all. When I need to "loosen up" the paint in the brush from time to time, I will, but otherwise I will work with the paint in the consistency it comes in from right out of the can. This might be too thick for some people, but it's fine for my purposes.

You might find that, even though you cleaned the surface well, you are still getting "fisheyes" in your paint from some sort of nearby contamination. HOK makes an additive for silicone inhibition called KE 170. It works like the enamel version called "Smoothie." Only use it if you have to. Once you use it, it must be used in all proceeding coats of paint in the final clearing or fisheyes will occur in the area where the additive was used.

1 Shot & Chromatic Lettering Enamels

"An alkyd-resin (oil-based), high-gloss enamel for interior or exterior use on metal, glass, wood or masonite. Intended for sign writing on store fronts, vehicles and wherever fine lettering work is desired." This is the company description of 1 Shot lettering enamels. A great, but short, description of a product that has been

This is all the 1 Shot line of lettering paints and additives you will need for use in pinstriping. The paint is an alkyd-resin (oil-based) high-gloss enamel made for outdoor sign use.

a big part of my life for many years. I remember 1 Shot being available, but in limited colors, when I started striping. Too bad that I found out years later that it was available at the same time I was trying to use house paint for striping cars. Oh well. We still use porch paint for background colors on some signs.

1 Shot and Chromatic product group, based in Gary, Indiana, are the leading product lines serving the graphic arts, sign industries, custom painters and pinstripers worldwide. Beginning in 1948, 1 Shot built a reputation for superior quality products. Today, these products are preferred by more sign and graphic artists than any other paint product.

1 Shot products include lettering enamels, art and sign poster colors, fluorescent colors and pearlescent colors. Industry preference for 1 Shot products is based on their excellent application properties and the wide range of colors that can be achieved. 1 Shot was the

pinstriper's replacement paint after the demise of the lacquer pinstriping paint manufacturer's product lines. Although 1 Shot dried slower than the stripers were used to, it still had all the colors that were normally available to them in the past. Because of this, the product line grew and in the mid 1990s new and bolder colors were added. The product line also added thinners, additives and a few tinting colors. Around 2000, Spraylat, 1 Shot's parent, company acquired the Chromatic Paint Company, thus strengthening it's product line even more.

Along with House of Kolor, 1 Shot is one of the few paint brands that makes most of its money selling 1/4-pint (118 ml) cans of paint. The larger sizes are less appealing because it's easier to store smaller amounts.

The company might not approve of this, but I have had a stock of 1 Shot enamels at my location in Germany since 1998. I've used the paints off and on all this time, and they still haven't gone bad.

1 Shot Additives & Reducers

Brush Cleaner: A premium product designed for conditioning, cleaning and storing brushes that have been used with 1 Shot oil-based paints. This product is intended for reconditioning, softening and renewing hardened, natural and nylon brushes. It has been specifically formulated not to interfere with the properties of oil-based sign paints.

Chromaflo: A flow enhancer that is an additive for enamels. It enhances vehicle solids, thus increasing gloss and durability of the final coating. If, after the paint film sets, it feels slightly "gummy," add a few drops of Chromasolv high temperature reducer to regain a proper working consistency.

Chromasolv High Temperature Reducer: A strong, slow reducer that retards the evaporation rate and allows for improved flow and leveling. It is also effective in aiding cure when painting in conditions of higher temperature and humidity.

Edge "The Sign Painter's Thinner": A pre-mixed combination of flow enhancer and reducer. This product is intended for larger-scale painting and lettering. The

single-component reducer/flow-enhancer combination makes it easy to keep paint flow up, especially when hand lettering larger-scale copy and graphics, as well as panels and backgrounds.

Hardener: Designed to accelerate dry time for all 1 Shot alkyd-based paints. This hardener will improve adhesion to most substrates as well as extend color life and increase gloss. It also aids in preventing lifting when an automotive clear coat is to be applied over the paint.

1 Shot Reducer, Low Temp Reducer, and High Temp Reducer: These are products intended to improve flow in normal, low-temperature and high-temperature conditions, respectively. These products adjust viscosity and evaporation rate without significantly altering the quality of the final coating. They are designed for use with all 1 Shot and Chromatic products.

Tinting Black & White: Tinting bases for use with lettering enamels and bulletin colors. These products help in achieving various color shades without affecting the properties of the base coating.

Other Reducers, Brands and Types

Thinning enamels requires great care when you are selecting any reducer outside of a particular paint system. In most cases, the paint companies will not warranty their own products unless you use their reducers. However, if you're not having trouble with what you're putting in the paint, then don't worry about it. Here are all the reducers or thinners that I know about. Some, frankly, work better than others.

DuPont 3864 "Vai-temp" and 3812 "fast" reducers: Made for the automotive paint trade, these old stand-bys of the body shop world have been used by stripers, including myself, for years. I heard it said once that "if you're going to put 1 Shot on an auto, then use auto paint reducer." There are other brands of automotive paint reducer on the market, but I don't know much about them. Consult your local auto body supply company about these products.

Mineral spirits: This product is commonly know as paint thinner, and is available at all paint, stores, paint departments, and even some auto parts stores. I don't recommend mineral spirits as it tends to allow paint to dry too fast.

Turpentine: Used by artist primarily to reduce oil paints. Great for use with 1 Shot and doesn't make the paint dry too fast. I used "turps" when I first started striping, and now every time I smell it it takes me back in time to the '50s. Ah, the memories!

Gasoline (aka benzene and diesel fuel): A witch's brew of chemicals, but it works to thin 1 Shot. Be very careful. Gas will make the paint dry very fast. Diesel should only be used sparingly to make the paint flow a little better. Don't expect diesel to thin the paint very well.

Lacquer thinner: Also use this sparingly. If you need to speed up the drying time on cold winter days, then use it. Just remember that it will cause 1 Shot to flatten out or "chalk" much faster. Don't forget that lacquer thinner is not a spray gun cleaner. In some states, body shop suppliers are not allowed to sell lacquer thinner. In California, for instance, you can only buy it in the paint department at hardware stores.

Additives

Japan Dryer: This is used for speeding up the drying time of enamels. Available at sign supply stores. Follow label instructions.

Silicone Inhibitors: Otherwise known as "Smoothie," this product by the Marson Corp. has been used for silicone inhibition in auto enamels for years. Follow instruction and use it sparingly. Once you use it in one color of paint in your designs or lines or both, you must use it in all proceeding paint colors being applied or the paint could fisheye or crater. This is very unsightly and could also cause some loss of adhesion of the paint to the surface.

Penetrol: Used by painters around the world to allow the enamel paints to dry at a slower rate. Great for reducing paint stroke lines. In warm weather, Penetrol is used to allow paint to flow from the brush easier, thus eliminating rough or "firred" edges on the lines.

Clear Coats & Varnishes

1 Shot and Chromatic group offers a complete line of clear coats and varnishes.

Clear Flattening Paste: This product incorporates a varnish additive that adjusts the gloss of enamels in a range from just off high gloss to matte through the addition of measured amounts of paste.

Clear Overcoat Varnish: Recommended as a final protective coat for gold leaf when applied onto glass. After shading or outlining is complete, clear overcoat varnish provides final protection. Can also be used as a mixing varnish for stains and other paints, and as a sizing when quick surface gilding is desired.

Fast Gold Size: A self-leveling and fast-setting sizing for use in gold leafing. Designed to retain elasticity, fast dry gold size allows gilding to begin in about an hour, and engine turning for up to an additional eight hours.

Sign Finishing Clear: A clear "finishing" varnish additive used to extend or to create glazes and transparencies when used with lettering and bulletin enamels. It is not recommended as a clear topcoat.

Sign Restoring Clear: An oil-based, clear finish formulated for sign restoration.

Speed-Dry UV Resistant Acrylic Clear: A multipurpose, solvent-based acrylic clear with ultra violet absorbers that help protect against color fading. This product is for interior or exterior use on PVC pressure sensitive vinyl, wood, Masonite, MDO plywood, drywall, metal, and plastic.

Other Clears and Varnishes

There are other types of clears in urethane, enamel, and varnish form. Here are most of them that I am aware of.

Other automotive urethane clears: Every auto paint company makes their own clears. Some of their hardeners or catalysts can be used in 1 Shot. I don't recommend using different hardener from outside one company's line of paints in the automotive field. This should never be done unless approved by a reputable source like a paint supply company. I recommend using automotive urethane clear over gold leaf. If it's on a car or boat and out in the elements, urethane clear is your best bet to protect it.

Another brand is Frog Juice. The original formulation of this acrylic enamel clear was made by DuPont Paints under the designation Sunscreen 7000. It's great for covering 1 Shot artwork or gold leaf.

Marine Spar Varnish: Used by most sign painters for covering gold leaf work. It's been used for years for fire truck leafing as well as signage on both vehicles and outdoor signs. The drawback to this product is that you *must* re-varnish the area once a year.

Paint Storage

Glass or plastic jars work best for storing your paint. The size of the jar should depend on the application. I use 1-ounce jars for my hardeners. You don't need to store any more than that or the hardener will get thicker and go bad on you. I use 2-, 4- and 7-oz. jars for paint. I mix my House of Kolor urethanes in 2-oz. jars when mixing hardener with the paint. The same with 1 Shot and its hardener. I don't trust paper Dixie Cups. Even the paint companies warn against using these paper cups. Four- and 7-ounce jars are what I usually keep my mixed 1 Shot paint in. For special colors that I mix up to match auto interior colors, I use mayonnaise jars. I can mix up a quart or more of a special color and not have to worry about running out of a special mix for many months to come.

There is a plastic bottle product called E-Z Pour that holds paint and works well for easy mixing. It comes in 4-, 8- and 16-once bottles that use the same size caps for all.

For cleaning up my brushes I have a 10 3/4-oz. jar at the ready full of thinner to wash out the paint. This jar comes from potato chip dips like Ruffles Onion or Frito Bean dip.

Plastic medical cups like the ones used in hospitals are good for holding small quantities of paint, but not good for storage. Dixie Cups in the 4-oz. size are used by a lot of sign painters for holding paint. This is the type I use for my pre-mixed paints. I'll put a little in a Dixie Cup and load my brush from there onto the palette.

Palettes

A simple slick paper magazine is the best palette I have ever found. Phone books are made with very porous paper and will suck up your solvent and vehicle from the paint faster than a top-fuel dragster runs the quarter mile. Back up that magazine with a clipboard from an office store.

A simple slick paper magazine is best for a paint palette. The clipboard is great for holding the palette still and keeping the pages in place.

Cleaning Up

If you're going to work with paints, you need to know how to clean up a mess. Effectively cleaning up a tiny mistake on a line you painted is almost an art form itself. Say you're going along on a straight line. Everything is flowing out nicely and then it happens — a hair or a piece of lint gets caught in your base line tape. You run over the hair with your brush and, wham, the line edge is all over the place. So what do you do? This is where a little finesse comes in. Break the tape at the nearest panel edge. Pull back the tape and expose the defective line to repair. Using a cotton rag or, better yet, a piece of T-shirt material wrapped around a popcycle stick, gently push back the paint away from the edge into the line, being careful not to go out into the opposite edge of the line. Do this correctly a few times and should be able to save the line from being a total loss. Of course, the other method would be to just wipe off the line and start over.

Cotton rags are relatively easy to come by. Terry towels, too. Most auto parts stores carry them, as well as the big discount and warehouse stores. I recommend terry towels for applying wax, grease removers and other forms of solvents needed to clean or prepare the surfaces for paint. However, if you're cleaning off something such as glue from a vinyl sign that was removed, use paper towels. Otherwise, you'll be throwing away cleaning rags with glue on them.

Sometimes you might have a little mistake on the line from misjudging or misplacing the beginning of a continuation of the line. Maybe it's from missing the start of a line connecting another line in a design on a deck lid or hood. Some people call these mistakes "spurs." These little spurs can be almost impossible to correct. They might be too small to get to, or too

close to another line. I found an Eberhard Faber plastic (vinyl) erasing pencil works very well for these fixes. These tools are also available under the Peel Off Magic Rub or Wipe Out Tool monickers.

Once you've got a mistake fixed, you'll find that there is a little paint residue left on the surface — sort of a light smudge of paint. What do you use to remove that last little bit of smudge? Skin oil, believe it or not. Just wipe a little skin oil from the side of your nose, and wipe away the residue of your mistake with a rag. Make sure to clean off any residue skin oils afterwards.

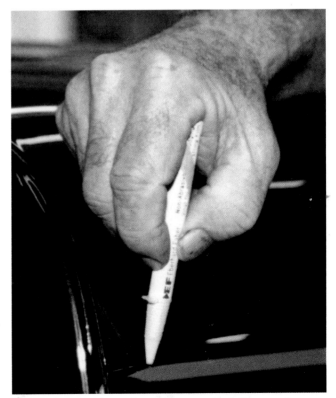

Several companies make vinyl erasers that allow you to "push" the paint away from the line.

Your Main Tool: The Brush

Without the right tool, you will never get any good work done in this trade. Finding the right brush is the most important thing next to learning how to use it. With nine companies offering brushes from squirrel hair to synthetic, finding the right brush can be a difficult task. When you first pick up a striping brush it can feel very strange. To me, and lot of others it feels, well, unnatural. It's not like holding a pencil. The brush takes a while to get use to it, but once you do get familiar with the feeling, you'll have that feeling for ever. I quit striping on a regular basis for about 5 years at one time in my life. When I picked up a brush again and started using, it took all of about five minutes to get used to it again. I will cover a lot more on using the brush in another chapter.

So, with all these companies offering brushes, which one would you pick? A good rule of thumb is to use a brush that you can find easily. Art supply stores, auto body suppliers, auto parts suppliers, sign suppliers and various Web sites are all good sources for striping brushes.

One company that stands out from all the rest for availability and overall variety is the Mack Brush Company of Jonesville, Michigan. The original striping brush was an elongated lettering quill called a striping pencil. The hairs were 2 1/2 inches out from the ferrel and the brush was held like a lettering brush. I recently saw an advertisement for BMW Motorcycles somewhere and, amazingly, the company was still using a striping pencil to do lines. Harley-Davidson uses a Beuglar tool device to stripe its tanks now.

There are four main parts of the brush. The handle, the wrap, the belly and the tip.

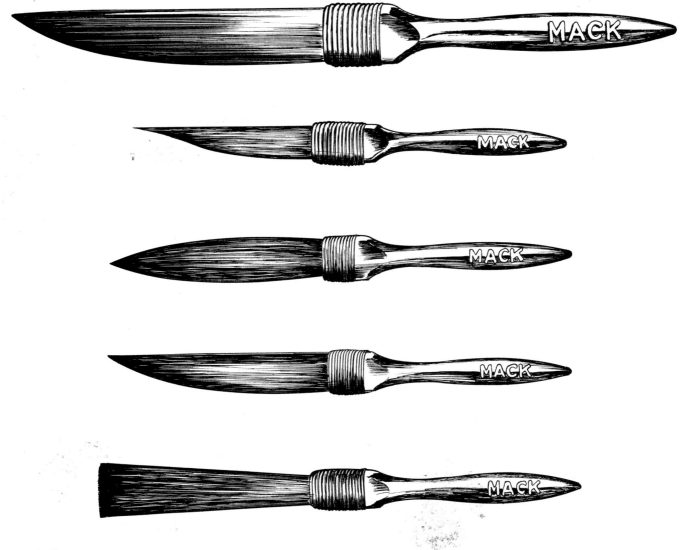

The Handle

The handle can be 2 1/2 to 5 1/2 inches in length and made of different woods (usually cedar), aluminum or even simulated pearl. Some handles are long to effect a steadier straight line, or to reach hard-to-get-at areas like wheel rims. Most handles are 2 1/2 to 3 inches. This shorter length allows for better turning and handling of the brush.

Some stripers really like the extra length. I prefer it myself. I have my own long handle brushes made for me by the Mack Brush Company for long line striping. They use an old stock of "Grip Stroke' and "True Grip" handles that were manufactured back in the 1930s. Other companies such as Sharf (England) or Fuestal (Germany) make long-handle brushes as part of their normal inventory.

Another variation of the handle was the Mack double liner striper. These were manufactured from around 1930 to 1960. The purpose of this variety of brush was to be able to do two lines of striping at on time. The brush was primarily for use in the auto factories and maybe even the carriage manufacturers. The width between the lines was specified by the company ordering the brushes. The size of the line width also varied from size #0 to #3. Loading paint into these brushes must have been a real chore until you got used to it. I've seen one being used. Once the paint is loaded into both brushes, a piece of paper or business card must be moved in between the brushes and then pulled through them to separate the two.

The Wrap, or Ferrule

The wrap or "ferrule" is the part that holds the hairs of the brush to the handle. Some wraps are metal, generally brass, pressed on with a machine. Others use garden twine or brass wire and are hand wrapped. Glue is usually applied before wrapping to hold the hairs in place. The older striping pencils used a cat gut ferrule to hold the bristles and were mated to a handle like the ones used with lettering quills.

The Hair of the Brush

The hair is obviously the most vital part of the brush.

There are two areas to keep be familiar with: the belly and the tip. The belly is the fattest section of the brush with the most hairs. Some brushes are made with a lot of hair in the belly to carry more paint for a long line. Some are thin in the belly and carry less hair to effect a finer and more uniform line, as seen in a pinstripe design or fine, long line.

The amount of hair and the shape of the tip of the brush determine the size of the line. If you were to take a 000 striping brush and cut too much of the tip off, it would give you the size line that 00 or even a 0 brush would give you — not a good thing if you plan to make a 000 line.

Brush sizes vary between manufactures. Most companies go up to #3 and down to #00. This is a variation of almost 1/4 inch in line width. Mack Brush not only makes a #4 size brush which will give you a 1/4-inch line, but also makes a series of brushes called "broadliners." These brushes are recommended for filling sectional areas, wide graphics and broad lines. These brushes range from #00 to #7 in size and will deliver lines as small as 1/4 inch to more than 1 inch. On the other end of the spectrum, the Xcaliber brush is made for striping alone and comes in sizes #0000 to #0. These brushes are great for designs and panel art. A #000 and #0000 Xcaliber will get your lines down to 1/32 and finer.

There are two types of materials that form the tuft of a brush:

Synthetics: These are man-made of either nylon or polyester. The hair may come tipped, tapered, flagged, abraded or even etched to increase the brush's ability to carry paint or color. The man-made filaments may be dyed and baked to make them soft and more absorbent. The advantages of a synthetic brush are: they are very durable; they are less likely to be damaged by moths, varmints, paints, or mild solvents; they are easier to clean and they work best for acrylic paint.

Natural: No animals are raised or trapped for the sole purpose of making a brush. Natural animal hair may be used in its pure state or mixed with other types of hair to accomplish a particular mixture for price, and or, performance. Natural hair will hold a tremendous amount of paint, because it has microscopic scales along the shaft of the hair. Quality and price of natural hair is determined by the grade of the animal, and by the supply and demand. Generally speaking, longer hair is harder to find and more expensive than shorter lengths.

Types of Hair

Squirrel Hair: Blue squirrel is the most readily available and comes in long and short lengths. It is generally used for striping and lettering brushes. Brown, or kazan, is no longer found in shorter lengths and used for stripers, quills, and outliners. Both the blue and kazan are very soft and fine. I've heard it referred to as the softest hair on earth. They "point" as well as a kolinsky, but have very little "snap," since the hair is not very resilient. Grey squirrel is the hardest to find and the most expensive. It is more durable, has more "snap", and makes a great quill or lettering brush.

So the question remains: Which brand of brush do you use? I have a preference for a Mack Series 10 myself, but that's just me. Mack makes 15 different configurations of striping brushes. Some are just good for straight lines, some for designs, and some for overall use. I been striping a long time and the choices are difficult for me to make, let alone a novice.

Mack Brushes

These products are of the best quality and highest standards, and I recommend Mack products to all who ask. The brushes are available in sizes 000, 00, 0, 1, 2, 3, and 4.

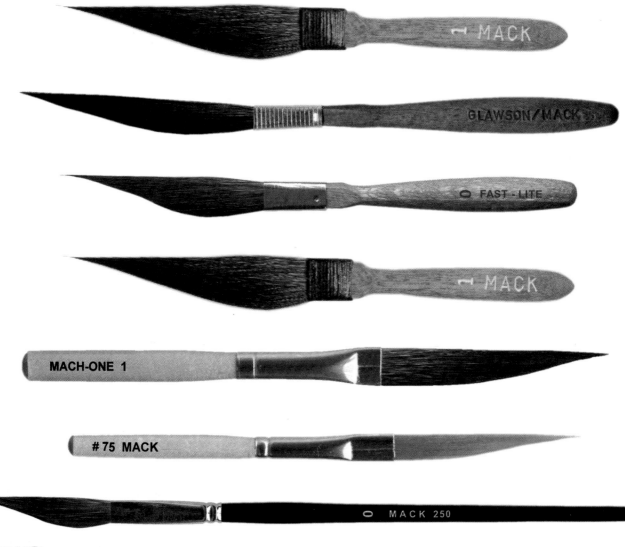

De Vinci-aka Cosmos

As described by the company, the 700 series brush has a long belly that makes it perfect for doing long, straight lines. The metal ferrule holding the hair is very narrow from the top to the bottom. Because of this narrowness, there is no room for the hair to bulge out in the middle resulting in greater control for the striper. The 701 series has shorter belly hair and makes this brush perfect for curls, turns and decorative work. The top end of the brush has the same hair length as the 700, but the under belly has shorter hair. Both series of brushes have cedar wood handles that are flat on the sides. The handle also has two grooves running around it. The brush is available in #0, 1, 2, and 3 sizes.

Hamilton and Handover

Both of these brushes are made by the A. S. Handover Co. of London, England. The Hamilton brushes are available in kasan squirrel and red sable. Their handles are the only ones made that hold the hairs of the brush on both sides of the wrap. Brush sizes go from #00, 0, 1, 2, 3, and 4. These are also the most expensive brushes for striping. Because of the limited quantity made by Handover, the retail price of these brushes is around $50 today.

The Handover line of brushes are not quite so hard to get, but their numbers are also limited. Brush sizes go from #00, 0, 1, 2, 3, and 4.

Kafka

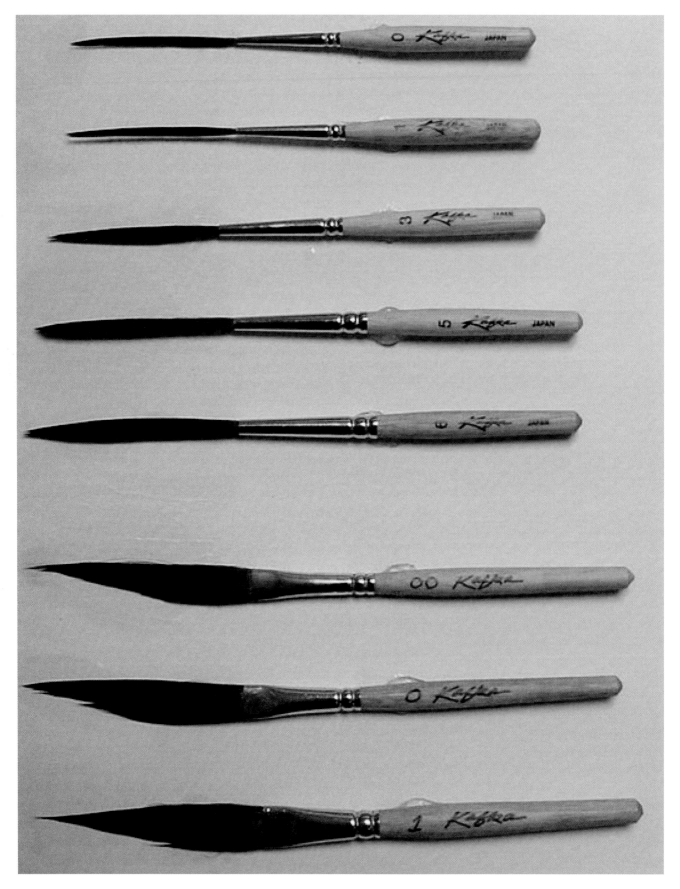

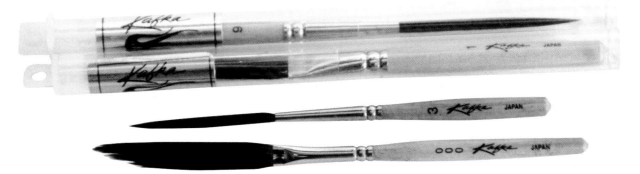

There are two distinctly different brushes in the Kafka line of products. One is for straight lines and one is for curves and scrolling. The straight liner is used for just that, straight lines only. The scroll brush is designed to do everything design-wise that any other striper will do, plus do scroll styles and do arcs and outlin flames with ease. Although this brush looks like a throwback to the era of the striping pencil, it works so well that many of the pros have given this brush rave reviews. Available is sizes # 0, 1, 3, 5, 6.

Luco

Also called a Leonard, this brush is made in France of Kasan squirrel hair. The handle is cedar and the ferrule is would with brass wire. It is the only brush made with a brass winding. Available in sizes #00 to # 5.

Leonhardy

As striping brushes goes, this is one of the good ones, although it's scarce. Not many distributors carry them and you will probably have to order them special. This is not a stock, company brush; dagger stripers only. They are made in Germany with squirrel hair, brass ferrule and colored cedar handle. Available in sizes #0 to #6.

Xcaliber

The Xcaliber striping brush is rated as one of the best brushes for design work, especially panel art. It's short hair length (1.5 inches out compared to most brushes that are 1.75 to 2.25 inches out), makes it particularly well suited for those short and long lengths of lines that make up a modern pinstriping design. The shorter length allows for much greater control of the brush consistency, and line size.

LazerLines

This is not just a brush, but a technology breakthrough in brush manufacturing. The LazerLines brush is many brushes with one handle. Lazerlines.com makes brushes and supplies the trade with lettering quills and other sign painter's supplies. The brush head screws into the aluminum handle that is made for the brush system. The brush heads are available in five different models and from sizes #00 to #4.

Scharf

This is called the Series 2190. Made from Kasan squirrel hair, this long-handled brush is excellent for straight lines, but not much on the turns. The hair is 1 3/4 inches out from the ferrule. It comes in sizes five sizes. I found the brush only in sign supply stores.

The Legendary Brushes

These brushes are out of manufacture but are legendary for their quality and handling ability. Some are being made today under other names and by other companies.

The **Dominican** striping brush was used by some of the finest stripers in the world. It was an unbelievable straight-line brush. It came in sizes #00, #1/0, #1, and #2. The #00 was great for fine, fine lines.

The brush on the top is representative of the so-called "German" striping brush. The brush in the middle is not very old, but is exactly like the old "striping pencils" of the last two centuries. The brush on the bottom has wire wrapping instead of a pressed brass ferrule. All three brushes are made by the Habico Brush Company in Germany

The so-called **German** striping brush was a Robert Simons made in West Germany. Thanks to David Ford of San Rafael, California (800-947-1389), the old world German striping brushes are back. He has these custom made by A.S. Handover in London. They are available in #00 to #4 sizes; Habico from Germany also makes a brush in the same sizes and closely resembles what I have always referred to as a "German."

The **Grumbacher 1010 series** was my first brush. This was the only brush I ever saw that was made with a plastic handle. The handle was flat on the sides. I remember Von Dutch saying one time that if he wanted to stripe a flat line he would use a Grumbacher. Dutch felt that the brush was no good because of this. The 1010 series could hold a really straight line though, no matter what Dutch said. It just wasn't too good for turning corners. Mack Brush Company picked up the brush line in 2002 and now manufactures the brush as the Mach One Striper. It comes in sizes #00 to #2.

Brush Oils

Like any other hair, including your own, brush hair must be taken care of or it falls out. Lack of cleaning around the ferrule or in the length of the hairs can make it hard to use if not totally unusable. When the hairs get stiff, you're dead in the water. Here are the preservatives available:

Wall Dog Brush Oil: For use with natural hair. This brush preservative is acid free and contains no detergents. Formulated to nurture and condition the brush hair to restore its natural oils. Designed primarily for pinstripers.

Excaliber Brush Preservative: For use with all natural hair. Environmentally safe, non-detergent formula and contains vitamin E. Washes out with mineral spirits.

Neatsfoot Oil Compound: Great for brushes when other products are not available. It can be found in drug stores, sign supplies and shoe stores.

Lard Oil: This preservative comes from the top of the can of solid lard cooking oil. It's great for keeping your brushes oiled up but does not condition the hairs the way that Wall Dog or Xcaliber oils do. Available through most sign supply companies.

Motor and Transmission Oils: Use these if you absolutely have to. They contain petroleum, acids, and detergents and can literally eat some hair over a period of time.

Trimming the Brush

Although most brush companies try very hard to give us a quality product, it's necessary to tweaking brushes from time to time. When either the belly or the tip need attention, cut cautiously.

If you want the brush to give you a blunt start on the line, then the tip hair needs attention. If the line seems too broad for the actual size of the brush, then the sides of the brush back to the ferrule is your target.

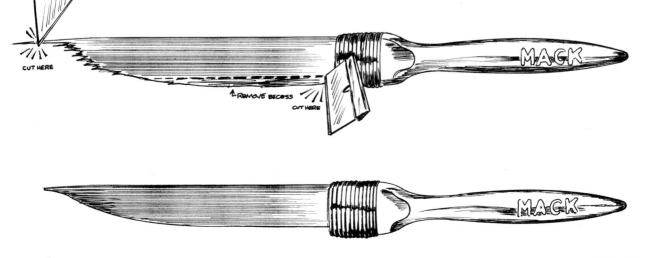

CUT HERE

REMOVE EXCESS

CUT HERE

MACK

MACK

Most of the trimming you will do nowadays will be in the tip and the arc of the sword shape of the brush. Trimming out the sides and the belly are no longer needed thanks to the re-invention of the Mack Series 10. Why do I make such a big deal of the shape and the amount of hair in these brushes? If you put too much hair in the belly area of the brush or don't watch how long the hairs are going out from the arc to the tip, you'll have problems making a good line. When the paint comes out of the brush, you should only be using about 3 to 10 percent of the tip to make the line.

The striping brush is shaped to carry enough paint to make a line 3 to 5 feet long. Some stripers like to pull a line down the whole side of a car, but it's hard to deliver the correct amount of paint to the line when you're 20 feet down the side of a car. Back when I could get the old #00 Dominican brushes, I could only pull a good, fine line about 1 to 2 feet without reloading the brush. Fine lines with a thickness of 1/64 inch or thinner must be heavy with paint if you're not burying them with clear. Otherwise, they won't stand the rigors of everyday wear and tear of the surface paint of a car. The Dominicans were a little too long on the tip, so I would snip a slight amount there, and then cut about 1/4 out of the bottom of the belly. The belly of these brushes was very short and had a tendency to "fishtail" the line when turning a corner. To stop this I cut out the bottom of the belly. This prevents any real short hairs from ruining your line.

Tool , Paint & Brush Boxes

The paint kit is the toolbox that stripers depend on. It should have enough storage room for our paints and assorted brushes and tools, it should be light and yet durable, and not cost a fortune. Some kits range as high as $400 or more. Most kits for the sign guys are between $85 and $195. Plano Molding Company has a wide array of tackle boxes that might fit your needs. They are available at most large sporting goods stores. D-Flite Products makes an all-aluminum box that a lot of sign painters use.

I use an ArtBin Brush Box. If you've ever been to an art store, you've probably seen these storage boxes. Some are small like a little toolbox and some are brush-storage size. Check them out at http://www.flambeau.com.

Make Your Mark

Back in the old days I saw numerous articles in *Hot Rod, Car Craft* and other car magazines about flame painting. The marking pencil they used was a "grease pencil" otherwise known as a China marker. They were easy to find and worked well for marking outlines of a flame layout. Chalk and charcoal sticks were the other, scratchy alternatives.

In the late 1960s a pencil product from Germany made by Schwan Stabilo called "Stabilo" arrived It's a water-based pencil product created by a company whose pens and pencils are know worldwide by most artists. This pencil is ideal for what pinstripers do. You can paint right over the mark as long as you don't leave too much of the pencil line on the surface. You should leave just enough to see what you're doing and no more. It comes in many colors; the easiest colors to remove are white and blue. It comes off with just the wipe of your finger or a rag with water or rubbing alcohol. It's available at some art supplies, and all sign supplies.

Another similar product is the Staedtler Lumocolor non-permenant pencil. It has all the same characteristics of the Stabilo and is also made in Germany.

Let's Go Shopping

There are many things that make up a striper's paint kit. Here's the inventory list of what I carry around.

Small funnel

Pair of heavy rubber industrial gloves

Dixie Cups

Pint can of brush oil

Marson "Smoothie" — 2-oz. bottle

3.5- and 7-oz. empty baby food jars

One color wheel

Various masking tapes and clear office tape

One cleaning brush (acid brush)

1 Shot color chip samples

Clipboard and extra magazines

Combination paint can-bottle opener

6- and 12-inch or 30mm ruler

10-foot measuring tape

Table knife (for cutting off the skins inside your paint cans)

Vinyl tape application squeegee

Small scissors

Exacto knife and extra blades

Plastic fork and plastic spoon

Olfa knife

Blue and white Stabilo pencils

Pencil sharpener

Single-edge razor blades

Craft sticks (popcicle sticks) stir sticks (12 inch)

Pair of tweezers

Small bottle of Elmer's Glue

Small bottle of "Super Glue"

#12 Griffold pounce wheel

Push pins

Pack of matches (for paint touch-ups)

Rubber garden knee pad

Bottle of glass cleaner

Roll plastic Saran Wrap

18- and 6-inch roll of 3M white masking paper

Red terry cloth shop towels

Various sponges (kitchen type, sea sponge & foam)

One gallon each of paint reducer, wax and grease remover and lacquer thinner.

One quart 5955 3M rubbing compound

One pint denaturized alcohol (shellac thinner)

Several plastic film cans (for special mixed paint color to give to the customer)

One plastic container of baby powder

One tack rag

One black and one white chalk pounce bag for patterns (store together in a plastic bag)

1/4 pints of pastel and seldom-used 1 Shot colors

Pint and quart cans of 1 Shot colors often used

1 Shot hardener and paint thinners

A full set of favorite pinstriping brushes for backup

Chapter Three

Going Straight

Since our last chapter dealt with brushes and paints, it might be a good idea before we go on to show you how to properly use these products. Every striper will have a different way of doing things. But the basics of mixing your paints, paletting and applying the paint are pretty universal. Psychology is also important when striping a line of any type. The thought in your head should always be, "I can do this."

Gerber baby food jars are great for storing 1 Shot or uncatalyzed House of Kolor Urethanes. The jars are available in 2.5-, 4- and 7-oz. sizes.

Mixing Paints

The first thing to know is the importance of following directions on the paint can. They are general and always recommend using their products. Obviously, from the description of thinners and other additives described in the last chapter, I don't go by the package directions myself.

I like using baby food jars when storing my 1 Shot paints. There are three different sizes available. The same jars are available in Europe, but I'm not sure under what brand name. In Germany the brand name is Hipp. We'll use a 4-ounce jar to demonstrate the mixtures of paint, Penetrol, thinner, and Smoothie that I used in a pre-mixed jar of 1 Shot.

This 4-ounce jar has the markings for paint, thinner and Penetrol.

Here are all the additives I put in my paint that is pre-mixed in baby food jars.

This is the factory-recommended combination of products to make 1 Shot withstand a urethane clearcoat

I like to pre-mix all my colors to save time. I never have liked the individual mixing procedure and I try to avoid it as much as possible. You, however, may like it. Take notice that I have added two black lines to the jar in the photo. The first line from the bottom marks the amount of 1 Shot to add. The second line marks the level for the Penetrol, and then above that you will add thinner. You can use mineral spirits or automotive enamel reducer. If you premix using 1 Shot reducer, Penetrol is nice to use occasionally, but not necessary. The last additive I use is Marson "Smoothie." This is used to prevent silicone craters, otherwise known as

House of Kolor makes a variety of pinstriping products. It's always best to stay within one paint system.

"pock marks." You may use 1 Shot hardener to step up the drying time and the adhesion factor. It will accelerate the drying process by 35 percent.

To mix 1 Shot for use under the clear coat, you must use only 1 Shot paint, thinner and hardener. If you're going to use clear over something, always stay within the "paint system." Do not deviate. You can also use a little Smoothie in the paint if necessary. Be sure to wash off the pinstriped area with 409 or wax and grease remover prior to clearing the surface. This gets rid of any silicone residue on the surface left from the smoothie. Drying time varies. The warmer it is, the better. Since 1 Shot is enamel, it will take a while to dry and it will water spot if the paint is not dry enough. To keep it from spotting after exposure to water, blow dry the water off the surface of the paint with high-pressure air and do not let the water dry on the tacky paint surface. This is what causes water spots.

House of Kolor Striping Enamel should only be mixed up on an individual basis. Premixing this product is not recommended. Always use HOK hardener when using this product. Generally, you will not need to use HOK thinner to reduce the enamel unless the paint becomes too thick in the brush or your are using it for airbrushing. HOK silicone inhibitor is also available. You can use HOK for surface striping or under the clear. If I need to get a job done fast, I use HOK for its quick drying ability. This paint dries in 5 to 15 minutes, depending on the weather. Once the hardener is added, it will be a matter of hours before the paint in the cup or jar dries to a solid. Be careful not to catalyze more than you need. Always follow the instructions for using this paint. If you mess up on a job using HOK, you might wind up having to pay for the whole job to get redone. This paint is not too forgiving. Be careful.

By the way, if you're striping a job that will go under the clear, always make sure that the painter has applied a "barrier coat," or intercoat clear, over the surface area you will be striping. You want to be able to wipe off a mistake without taking the base coat with it. Some painters will stripe right on top of the base coat. It's possible, but you can't make any mistakes.

When loading your brush with paint, work the brush back and forth in a mopping motion, loading it with paint all the way up to the " heel," or ferrule.

The last move in paletting the brush is running it over the palette a few times to adjust the tip. This motion takes the sharpness away from the tip of the brush.

You can be sure pre-mixed paint is free of any pieces of hardened paint by straining it into a paper cup before using it.

Let's Get Loaded

Getting paint properly into the brush is the most critical process in pinstriping next to actually pulling the line. Loading up your brush, also called "paletting," is not something you do gently. It is the act of getting the proper amount of paint into the hairs of the brush by stroking the brush side to side in a back-and-forth motion — sort of like mopping.

A palette can be a piece of paper from a glossy magazine (my favorite), or maybe a phone book page. By using a sort of flopping motion you work the paint into the hairs until the proper consistency is achieved. The paint must get all the way up in the brush to the ferulle. The last move in paletting is running the brush over the palette a few times to adjust the brush tip. If you don't do this, the tip tends to provide a very pointed start to the line. By paletting the brush tip a few times you give the start of the line a more blunted start.

Some stripers like to take the paint right out of the can and have a small cup of thinner nearby to mix into the brush to get that perfect feel. I prefer pre-mixed paint; that way you are always breaking up the thickened paint in the upper area, opposite the tip, by mixing in the pre-thinned paint. It's a production method I learned years ago when I was striping multiple units a day.

Be sure that your pre-mixed paint is free of pieces of hardened paint in the jar, and strain the paint if necessary. The consistency of the paint should be the same as 30-weight oil for designs and turns and a little

thinner for long lines. Penetrol helps the flow of the paint from the brush by not letting the paint dry too fast and cause a condition called "firring," or "spurring." Once you start practicing you'll find a favorite paint consistency one that works well for you. Whatever you do, be patient! Don't get ahead of yourself and load the brush wrong. You'll just be wiping the line off and starting over again.

Remember that you have to get the right feel of the paint in the brush. When I started, my mentor taught me that I would soon be able to feel the paint in the brush — actually feel it! I thought he was crazy until one day it actually happened. You'll be pulling a line one day and the consistency goes bad and you will "feel it." When this happens, stop, lift the brush, reload and start over. This will help you with consistency.

Ah yes, consistency. That's another thing. Always make sure you get enough paint thickness in the line. What I mean is, have the right amount of paint in the line for it to wear well over the years. This will come with practice.

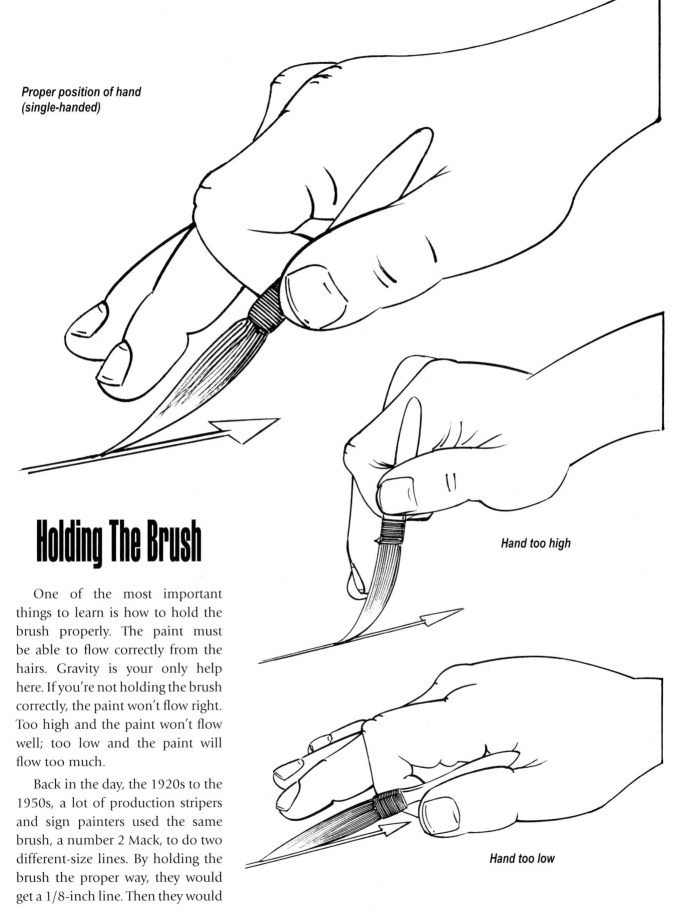

Proper position of hand (single-handed)

Hand too high

Hand too low

Holding The Brush

One of the most important things to learn is how to hold the brush properly. The paint must be able to flow correctly from the hairs. Gravity is your only help here. If you're not holding the brush correctly, the paint won't flow right. Too high and the paint won't flow well; too low and the paint will flow too much.

Back in the day, the 1920s to the 1950s, a lot of production stripers and sign painters used the same brush, a number 2 Mack, to do two different-size lines. By holding the brush the proper way, they would get a 1/8-inch line. Then they would

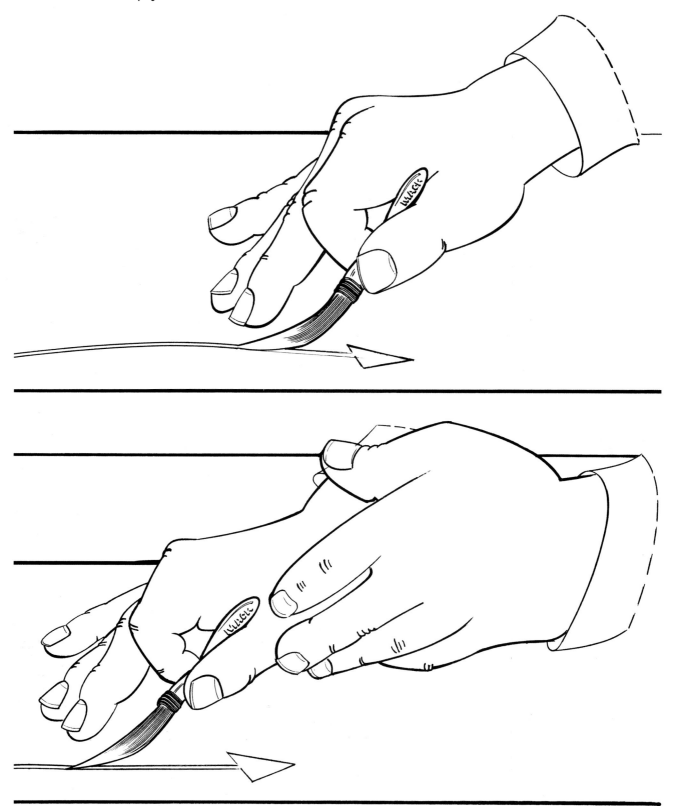

re-load the brush, "climb on the tip" using only a small percentage of the tip, and get a 1/16-inch or finer line with the same brush. Still, I'm a big believer in the adage "the right tool for the right job." Use the correct size brush at all times.

There are two ways to hold the brush correctly. You can use one hand or two. One-handed is the usual way most stripers work until they feel that they need a little steadying from the other hand. This happens when you're applying designs or going around a corner. It's like steadying your hand when you hold a gun — two hands are better than one.

Tommy the Greek was famous for his elongated scallops with "half lance head" points and teardrops.Later, painters graduated to scallops and panels, fade painting, and decades later, graphics.

What is a Bodyline?

A bodyline is an accent line that defines the "lines" of an object. If it were a car, you would first identify the most prominent feature of the side, rear end or hood areas. The same goes for a truck body, van, SUV, or boat. Bodylines could also be defined by their boxy appearance, as you would have on a tool, machine, or weight scale.

Bodylines come in different sizes and configurations, from a single 1/16- to 1/8-inch line, to a multitude of lines, stacked one on top of another, to thick lines outlined by another pair of lines. Whatever the configuration, its primary purpose is to bring out the line or shape of the object. Once we get into pinstripe design, we will cover this subject more in more detail.

On a cart, chariot, horseless carriage or other vehicle box lines were the first standard of decoration for hundreds of years. This is still true on today's carts and carriages. Most are simply outlined, however, mainly due to the lack of qualified stripers working today.

As late as the turn of the millennium replacement striping "repairing lines from the factory" could account for as much as half of the income of a pinstriping shop; more if the pinstriper could also do tape pinstriping.

In my career, over the last 27 years of operation in California, the amount of replacement striping in the body shop industry has risen and fallen dramatically. This is due to the ever-changing look of the "Detroit iron" available from year to year.

Over the last few years, my business in replacement pinstriping has been good due to Chrysler and Dodge minivans and Jeep Cherokees. Before that, it was Ford Tauruses and Mercury Sables. And then were the Cadillacs. The cars are always changing, and thus the need for replacement striping changes with it.

In general, the lines on the side, rear end and hood of a car are suitable for feature. It's hard to define the lines on some cars. The designers of some vehicles were obviously not interested in someone bringing out the lines of the car. It's not all that difficult to tell which models are right for accenting. Maybe you have seen how a body can look so much better with just a couple of lines added to it. My customers often comment that they can't believe how much a few lines change the look of a car.

Some vehicles are so devoid of lines that they look like "used bars of soap." The Mazda Miata is a great example of a body that needs a lot of help. The Chevrolet Corvette C5 model needs help in the upper body sections, and where the "cove" area is more defined, but still lacks definitive edges. Most vehicles you will tackle will have this semi-defined look.

"Modern" pinstriping first started getting popular in the 1950s, which was not a great era for defining a bodyline on a car. Tommy the Greek's "teardrops" were in great demand in the Oakland-San Francisco Bay area, and Von Dutch-style designs were popping up all over. But these were not bodylines. Painters started using scallops and flames. Later, they would graduate to scallops and panels, fade painting and, decades later, the modern graphics we see today.

The scallops used by Tommy the Greek were elongated with one point and "half lance heads" on the end towards the front. This type of shape usually defined the upper part of a panel or fender, and sometimes the line on the hood. Upside-down "T" shapes could be used on the deck lid or the hood. These scallops sort of floated free, but did a nice job of defining an otherwise rounded line of the panel. To this day, I am still purveying that Tommy the Greek-style of striping. Call it old school, nostalgic, or traditional, but it still works today for late model cars like Camaros, Mustangs and even Miatas.

Since we're talking about lines and defining the body of a vehicle, let's not forget about the abstract "Fresno Look." I have seen a lot of variations of layout of lines in my life, but I have never seen any style like this one. This look comes from the Central Valley area of California from Bakersfield to Sacramento. We first saw it emerge around the beginning of the 1960s. This style completely redefines the lines of a vehicle and cuts it up to change a car's lines entirely. Quarter lines and panels were the elements involved in the beginning of this trend. Later, in the '70s, the style evolved into "mini-graphics." Accent lines as thin as 1/100 inch are also used to run parallel to, or sometimes inside, the quarter lines. Tiny fine line filagre such as curls and scrolls adorned the lines in various locations.

Finding the Bodyline

The best way to identify a bodyline is to step back away from the object to be lined and take a good, hard look at it. Do the lines show up readily, or are they hiding? Some lines are very straightforward. Others need a little attention to wake up the object. Whatever the case, the process starts by taping off the car with guideline tape.

This 1969 Camaro is crying out for bodylines.

The average placement for guidelines is 3/4 inch below the crown of the fender and quarter panel.

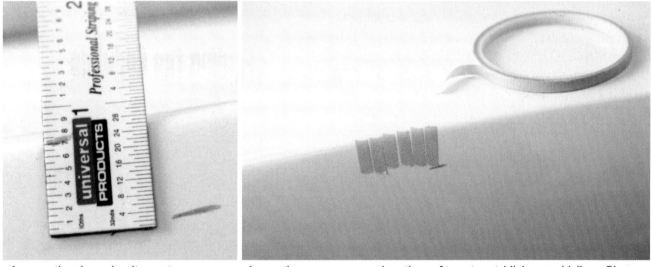

A magnetic ruler makes it easy to measure the distance for each mark for the guideline tape. This method can be used for striping with a Beugler tool as well as a brush.

I sometimes use measured sections of tape to establish my guidelines. Place your marks about every 6 inches to 1 foot apart.

Let's imagine that we have a 1969 Camaro to stripe and we want to establish a bodyline on the side of the car. The average placement for such an application is usually from 3/4 to 1 inch away from the crown of the fender, door and quarter panel of the car. I use 1/4-inch tape for my guideline, but you could use 1/8-inch to 3/4-inch wide tape. It's the striper's preference so, whatever feels good, do it. Establish a mark for your guideline with a Stabillo pencil. These marks are known as "tick" marks. Sometimes, I'll use measured sections of tape to establish my guideline.

Place your marks about every 6 inches to 1 foot apart to make sure you have enough of a visual guide to set up your tape. Pull out the tape about the length of the fender to start. Be careful not to pull too hard on the tape as it will stretch and become crooked and unusable. Tack down the beginning of the tape at one end of the car. If you're right-handed, you will probably start at the front of the left fender and reel out the tape to the back of the car. Use the same method on the right side, but start at the end of the quarter panel and reel out the tape to the front of the right fender. Do the opposite if you're a lefty.

Pull your guideline tape out the length of the panel your are taping to start. Be careful not to pull the tape too hard or you'll stretch it. Lay the tape down by tacking it at one end of the panel and slowly letting it down on the surface until you get to the end. It takes more time to get guidelines smooth on panels with arcs, like this one.

Here's a little trick: If you're not happy with the placement of your guideline, lay another piece of tape down where you would like it and then move the original tape into place just over or under the corrected line.

This model Camaro has a very "rolling" style of bodyline. Most other vehicles that you will be striping have a more straightforward line and are easier to layout. A good example of that would be a PT Cruiser's bodyline. It's simple, straightforward, and you can even run your finger in the little concave area of the bodyline.

"Gunsighting is the act of going to one end of a line and looking down it to the end to see if it is straight. If you see one end is wrong, take a line of tape and tack it to the surface parallel to the first line of tape. Make your correction with the second tape line and then move the first line next to it in the correct position. This also works for cleaning up arced layout areas for a graphic job or quarter line.

Painting The Line

Once you have your guideline established, it's time to mix the paint. If you're using 1 Shot Sign Enamel and my method of pre-mixed paint in a Gerber jar, take your brush and dip it into the paint. Get it on to the palette and work the paint into the brush. The paint, once loaded, should be the consistency of 30-weight motor oil. As you apply the paint with the brush, add a little paint thinner from time to time to the paint mix. I usually use a plastic bottle with a twist lock. These are available in drug stores. I add just a few drops at a time to "loosen" the paint up and then palette some more paint in the brush. Your paint will have to flow very well out of the brush in order to get a consistent line.

Here are some of the common painting problems you may run across:

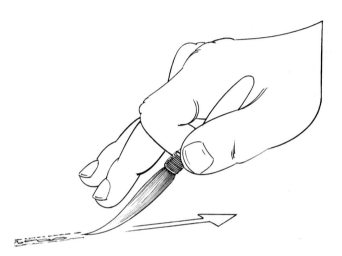

"Blobbing" *is when the paint dries up in the brush and causes an inconsistent amount of paint to be released. Add Penetrol and/or thinner to correct this.*

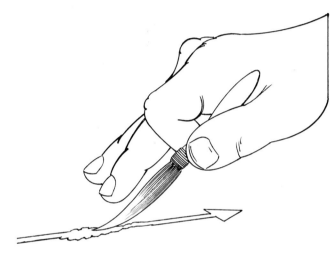

"Holidays" or " dry brushing" *occurs when the paint dries up in the brush and won't come out evenly. In this case, reload with more pre-mixed paint and palette well. Work the thinned paint up into the heel of the brush. This is where you will find the most dried-up paint.*

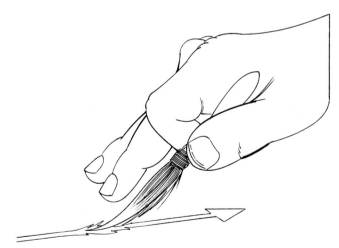

"Furring" *is similar to blobbing, with the paint resembling the way needles stick out on a fir tree. Add Penetrol and/or thinner to correct this.*

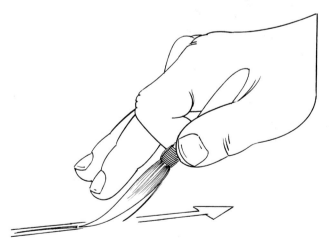

Loosing hairs *from your brush into the line is a real pain. It happens all the time, but you can help your own cause by keeping a very close eye on the tip of your brush. If you lose a hair in the line, stop immediately and, while the paint is still wet, take the tip of your brush, get under one end of the hair, and gently lift it up. You can then grab it with the tips of your fingers and remove the hair from the line.*

Practice, Practice, Practice!

Before you ever go putting any paint on someone's vehicle, you should have had many hours of practice doing these lines on your practice glass. I recommend a flat piece of glass about 3 feet long. Auto wrecking yards have these available at reasonable prices. Lay the glass flat on a bench or table first, then practice with the glass at 90-degree angle using two 2 x 4's to hold the glass. Practice straight lines, right-to-left s-curves and the mirror image of those curves, right-hand turns and left-hand turns.

You should also work on circles. Start at the right side and then do the left side, making sure to pull one line into the other so you can't tell where the line stopped and started. To pull a stripe to the left I use two hands — one to hold the brush and one to steady the brush hand. For right turns I simply pivot on my third and fourth fingertips. When turning a corner always lift slightly and twist the brush in a rolling motion. Use the brush like a rudder of a ship. Always turn the brush in the direction the line, flame edge or design is going.

Big Al Meadows, my illustrator for this book, holds a piece of auto glass used for practicing pinstriping.

To hold your practice glass, get two pieces of 2 x 4, 16 inches long, and cut grooves in them, one at 90 degrees and the other at 45 degrees. Make sure they are cut in the same place on each board.

Practice making straight lines and curves, both flat and elevated on a 90-degree angle.

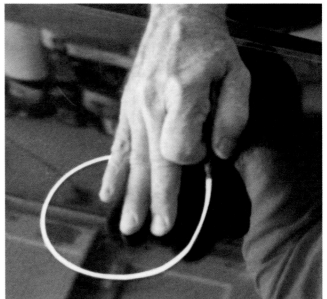

Work on circles going left to right and right to left. Start by doing this with the glass flat to the table. Practice multiple lines parallel to each other, one outside the other.

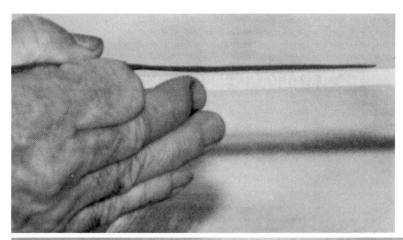

The "underhanded" method is preferred by most stripers.

The "overhanded" method is less popular, but still used by some stripers.

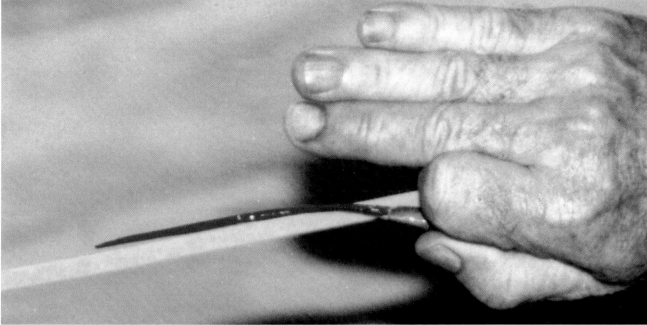

One decision you'll need to make is whether to stripe your straight lines underhanded or overhanded.

Underhanded is when the tape guideline is under the actual painted line. You will run your second finger on the bottom edge of the tape and hold the brush with your first finger and thumb. The other three fingers are held flat on the tips to act as a steadying device.

Overhanded is when you use your hand to hold the brush above the tape guideline. I generally use this method to get around objects like door handles and hinges.

When you start a straight line across a panel, always run the line from one end of the panel to the other. Don't stop in the middle. If you do have to stop in the middle, restart 6 inches back into the line. This will allow the brush to conform to correct size of the line as it comes out to the unstriped area.

When bringing one line into another from the opposite direction, as in the case of avoiding a door handle, stripe the line overhanded on one side to a point beyond the obstruction and then back in the opposite direction until the two lines meet. This sounds easy, it will require some practice to make it work. When you bring the line from one side to the other to make them join, use your peripheral vision. Paint the line to about 4 to 6 inches before they touch and then focus on the line you will be joining with. If your eye-hand control is hooked up right, your peripheral vision will take the line directly into the other with no evidence where the lines joined.

Always look directly at the line. Look at the tip and not the line before or after the tip. Concentrate on the variance between the line and the edge of your guideline tape. Keep the line around 1/32 inch away. Your brush acts like an airplane with all the changes an airplane can make: yaw, pitch and roll. Practice on glass first. Practice, practice, practice! Then go out and stripe everything in sight.

Starting On The Car

So, back to pulling that line down the side. With your hand properly placed on the tape guideline, start pulling the line as close to the tape as you can without actually touching it. If the paint gets on the edge of the tape it will probably "bleed" underneath the tape and cause a problem. Just go back and clean it up later. You want to stay so close to the line is to keep the line straight. Once again, using your peripheral vision, staying close to the line helps keep the line straighter. Don't move too fast. This is no race. Take your time and be patient with yourself and the brush. The more you practice, the faster you get. The second line will probably take longer than the first.

And what about lines inside the door jambs and

When outlining graphics, you will sometimes need to go inside the door jambs.

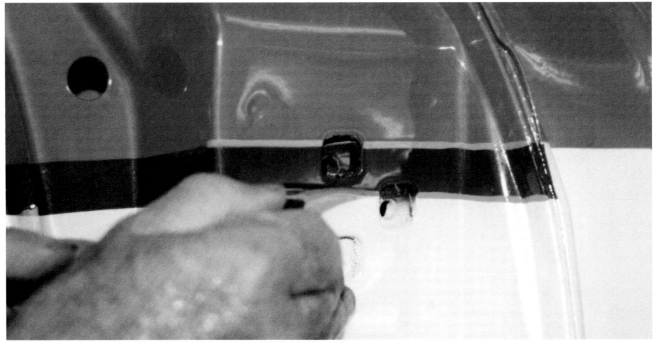

Use the brush the standard way to do longer lines in the jambs.

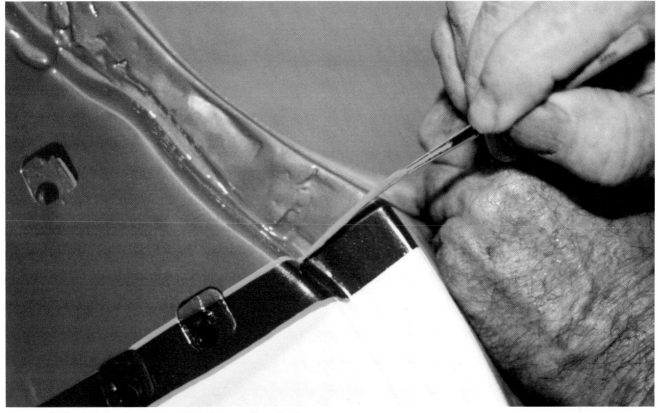

I use a Kafka Striping Brush to get into the smaller, shorter areas.

under the hood and truck lid? You'll have to do this to outline graphics if they continue into the jamb areas. It requires a whole new set of skills to get the brush to go over the various bumps and crevasses you'll encounter. One trick I use is to turn the striping brush upside down. It acts like a lettering quill and makes it easier to stop and start the line more bluntly. Use the brush the standard way to paint longer lines inside the jambs.

One option here is to use a Kafka striping brush. This swirley Q brush not only spins great circles, but is also very good for getting in tight places like jamb areas.

So, how many lines you should use when defining a bodyline? Here's where the aesthetics come in to play. Double lines, whether they are the same size or two different sizes, are the most common. Triple lines can be all the same size, or have a bigger one in the middle.

I always let my customer make the final decision on what to do with the lines, and for that matter, the whole job. If you're doing your own car, it all comes down to your own personal preference. ⌁

Chapter Four

Painting Lines Without A Brush

The last chapter dealt with painting lines using a brush, a baseline or guideline, and some good old-fashioned practice. It could be years, as in your humble author's case, before these very straight lines begin to happen. It does take a lot to get it straight and you might not want to wait. There are other alternatives to help speed things up.

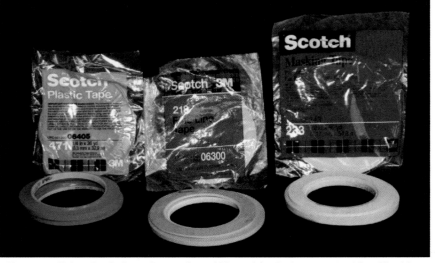

Here are all the plastic-based tapes from 3M used for laying out graphics. The blue tape turns well on corners, but the second green color tape will not. On the right are paper-backed. All are available in 1/4-inch and 1/8-inch widths. The green tape is available in smaller sizes.

Stencil Tape

The history of this type of product is well chronicled in the video *How to Pinstripe by Eddie Paul*, circa 1983 and 1984. Both versions featured a tape product made by 3M. To make a 1/16-inch line you simply pulled out one of the pre-cut lines of stencil tape on the roll. I believe it had six or more 1/16-inch lines already pre-cut. All you had to do was pull out as many lines as you needed and you were good to go. Yeah, right.

The problem was the tape was notorious for letting the paint bleed under it and making a real mess of your straight line.

By the time I got back together with Eddie and started researching what stencil tape product was out there, I had found out that 3M had discontinued the tape it had sold in earlier days and was making its own "fine line" series of green and blue plastic tapes. These would not allow paint to creep under the tape as long as you pressed the edges down firmly to form a seal on the edge. Today, you can still use this method to make lines as straight as a string down the side of a car. Here's how:

My plan when setting up my own stencil tape is to lay down a certain size of line first (1/4 or 1/8 inch),

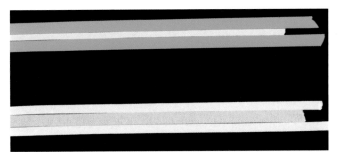

Using the 3M green or blue tape for laying out a 1/4- and 1/8-inch lines involves first laying down paper tape and pulling it up after the sides have been applied.

Once you pull out the center line tape, you'll have a perfect 1/4- or 1/8-inch line.

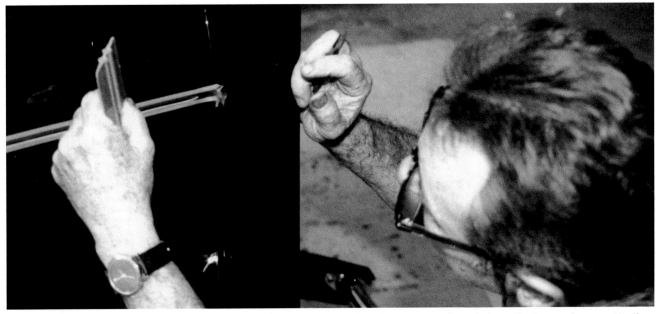

Once you have applied the Finesse Tape to the surface, be sure to take a squeegee and mash down the inner edges next to the paint. Use your fingernail if you don't have a squeegee.

and then use the corresponding tape to make sure then entire length of the line is exact and uniform. I do this exercise when I lay out a 1/4-inch line, or "quarter line," for a "Fresno-style" job.

The other way you get stencil tape is to actually buy it. Wow, what a concept. There's a company in New York named Finesse that manufactures tapes of varying sizes for striping straight lines. The tape has a very uniform physical width (about 3/4 inch), and has pre-cut centers. The tape comes in 42-foot and 160-foot rolls and 63 different precut varieties of line width and combinations of widths. The company has selected some of the various sizes to match original factory pinstriping. It's great for body shop pinstripe repairs, and I've even seen a few trick line ends made from this tape.

Finesse also makes a tape similar to 3M's fine line series called the "Edge." This tape is a real time saver for my 1/4-inch line jobs. I do a lot of these on street rods and PT Cruisers. First, start by laying down the tape in

the selected area. Once you have applied the tape, go back over it with a good vinyl application squeegee to mash down the edges. If you don't have a squeegee, use your thumbnail. The tape comes with a clear application film on top to allow smooth delivery of the tape to the surface. The application tape can be hard to separate from the Finesse tape on the surface. I either scrape the tape away from the application tape with my fingernail, or use a pair of tweezers to pull the two apart. I also use the squeegee or fingernail technique again to go over the tape and push it down again after removing the application tape. Make sure all the edges are down before painting a line in the center of the tape. You don't want your edges bleeding through.

If you are using House of Kolor urethane striping enamel and not 1 Shot, scuff up the surface to be painted first by using a red Scoth Brite pad. Clean off the dirt and lint from the surface using a tack rag. Check the surface afterwards for any residue.

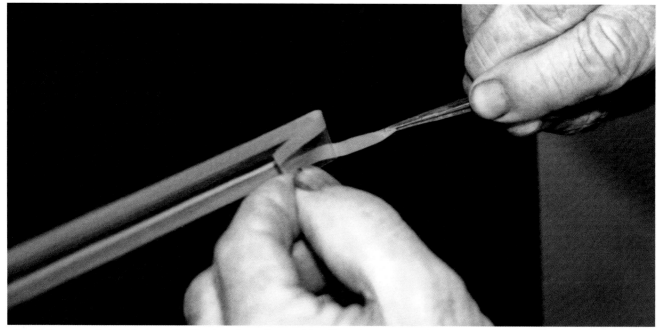

Carefully separate the clear application tape from the masking. I'm using tweezers here to get the job done, but you can pull it back using you fingernails.

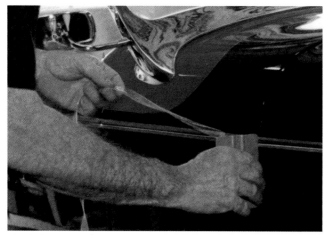

Pull the application tape off slowly so you don't pull up part of the surface tape.

When painting in the lines, be careful to mash the Finesse Tape edges down again just before you start to paint. The color can easily bleed under edges that are not sealed.

Then you can start painting in the line. Check the edges of the tape as you go along for holidays**.** At the beginning and end of each line, I recommend finishing the line by "cutting in" a straight edge of paint. After painting in the line, remove the tape edges. If you're using 1 Shot, wait for 10-15 minutes after applying the paint before removing the tape. Sometimes the enamel will not be quite dry enough and will form strings of paint after you pull up the edge. If this happens, clean things up before outlining the edges. Once you have all the tape off and you have checked all your paint edges, go ahead and pick a line size to border your stripe.

Stencil tape definitely makes this process easier.

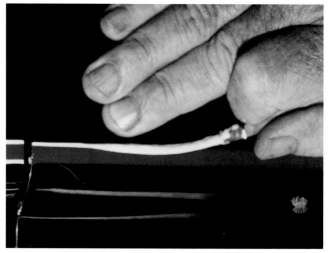

A #00 or #000 brush can be used for outlining the edges.

Clip Art Stencils

Around the mid 1990s, a few companies started paying royalties to pinstripers who created their own pinstripe design line of computer clip art. Vector Art of Pacific Grove, California, was the first and others soon followed. Artist like Bob Bond, Mr. J, and Steve Kafka have their own series today and the product, even though a facsimile of the real thing, has its place in modern pinstriping and signs. I wouldn't be caught dead with this stuff in my shop, by you might want to use it in stencil form until you feel comfortable enough to put down your own designs. Vector Art is still in business and has a wide variety of designs in graphics, antique panels and ornaments, cartoons and design elements, in addition to pinstriping examples.

Even though Bob Bond had a design line with Vector Art, he and Bob Iverson developed a vector-based line of clip art called "Splash Mask" Graficconcepts. The clip art was all graphic designs developed by the two men and offered the user the ability to resize the graphics to any length and height. I have personally used this product. I have also juggled one element in from another design and created some designs of my own. It's a little tedious, but fun, too. Splash Mask is now part of the Vector Art "Mega Collection #1." It's still called Splash Mask and contains purely ornate and antique designs. Golden Era Studios has a few CDs out, too, with loads of great art, as does a company called Butler Gold.

To use art from a disc, you will need either a sign company that will cut your masks for you, or your own setup, which can be rather costly. When I decided to branch out from hand-painted pinstriping and signs into the wide world of vinyl sign graphics, I found the cost to be a little alarming. If you don't plan to get into the business fulltime, I would suggest making friends with a local sign artist or franchise sign company that has the cutters and can make your stencils for you. I found that buying the software to run the clip art can be expensive. And then there's the cutter machine, which is known as a "plotter." Costs on these machines that only cut, but don't print, have come down considerably since my first journey into computer-aided signs. Still, if you don't want to get into a lot of expense, find a sign guy or company that can help you out.

The Beugler Tool

If you've ever been to a car show, then you've probably seen a Beugler Tool. All the large shows have a least one guy selling "the tool." It has its place, especially for industrial strength applications like trailers for heavy equipment and horse trailers — places where the surface will take a lot of abuse and not get much more care than an occasional wash job with a pressure washer. Lately, house and faux painters have been using the tool when they can't find a professional striper to do their work. So, what is it and where did it come from?

Samuel Beno Beugler was born in Tennessee in 1890, lived in Oklahoma for some time, than moved to Los Angeles in 1929, where he opened Beugler Auto Reconstruction did bodywork, mechanical services and welding. He did some work himself using a striping brush, but felt he needed to provide the trade with another way to get the lines on a vehicle or other surface. He developed a revolutionary device that didn't drip or run and provided paint on demand with accurate lines. He began to manufacture the tool in 1933.

He patented his design in 1935 and kept the business growing with new inventions, including parking lot and basketball court stripers. Beugler passed away in 1966 and his grandson took over the company.

In the late 1960s when the auto manufacturers went back to striping their cars, they needed a way to put a line on the cars using automation. So Beugler, and later other manufactures, invented a tool to do this striping, on the assembly line, using a metal guide to assure the consistency of the lines.

The original Beugler Tool looks nothing like the ones used at the auto factories. The only thing that's the same is the idea of a tube to hold the paint and the striping wheel itself. I tried unsuccessfully for months to find a picture of the. I've heard that the guide is an aluminum tube setup that is attached to the car using air and suction cups. Whatever they use, I've done my share of fixing and repainting factory lines. I just grab my brush and carefully stripe right over the top of the original line. Considering how quickly they must do the line at the factory, they manage to keep it very consistent and straight, especially on the Cadillacs.

I find the little thing intimidating. I've tried to use the Beugler Tool at car shows, and have even been instructed by a salesman from Beugler on how to use it.

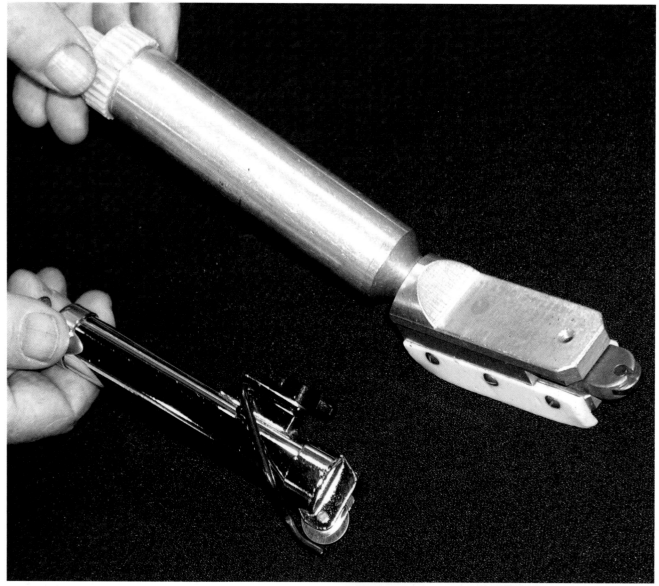

The Beugler Tool to the left is available to the public. The one on the right is the auto assembly line version.

He made it look so easy. This fellow wasn't available to write an explanation of how to use it, so I turned Gary Jenson, a friend of mine and fellow striper from Salt Lake City. Jenson is an expert with this tool. Following is his tutorial.

Using The Beugler Tool and Creating A Stripe

1 Lay down a 1/4-inch tape as a guideline to follow. You may want to double-layer the tape for the first few jobs to get the feel for it.

Lay down a line of 1/4-inch tape for a guide line.

[Author's note: I have also seen 1/2- and 3/4-inch tape used. Some people use the magnetic guide for making the line straight. Others, like Gary, just use a smaller tape as if you were running a brush line next to your guide. To make sure that you understand all the materials and parts of the tool and its use, I recommend picking up the video from Beugler.]

Load the Beugler with unthinned 1 Shot paint.

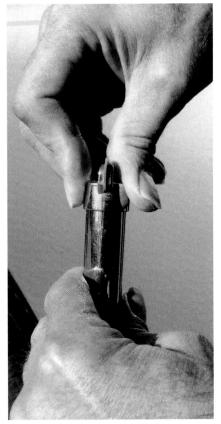

Securely place the head back on the tool, making sure it is lined up straight.

Push down the plunger until you see the paint start to come out of the little hole in the wheel head.

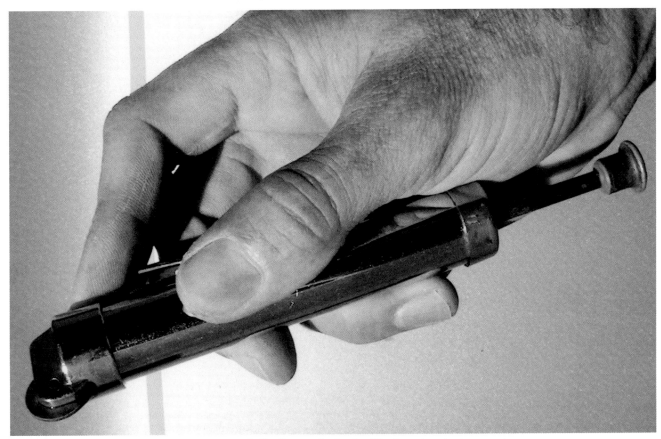

Hold the Beugler Tool like you would a carpet knife. Secure the back of the barrel against your palm.

2 Load the Beugler with *unthinned* 1 Shot paint. Be sure the plunger extends out 2 inches when the tool is full of paint. This will be explained later.   Securely place the head back on the tool, making sure it is lined up straight.

3 Push the plunger until you see paint starting to come out of the little hole in the wheel head.

4 Hold the Beugler like you would a carpet knife. Secure the back of the barrel against your palm. Notice how the plunger extends past the palm so you don't accidentally push it in as you stripe. This can become very messy.

5 The photo below shows two lines on the 1/4-inch tape. These are "priming lines." You do this to get the paint started on the wheel. Place the wheel about 1/8 inch away from the edge of the tape and start to pull the line down the side of the vehicle. Some people like to work under the line of tape; others work above it. Do whichever is most comfortable.

Place the wheel about 1/8 inch from the edge of the guideline tape.

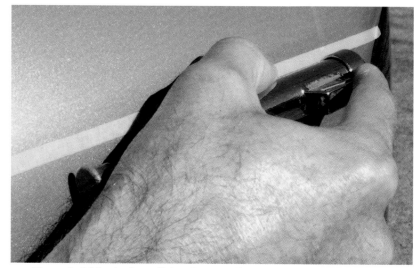

Always hold the tool parallel to the tape. If you don't, it won't go straight.

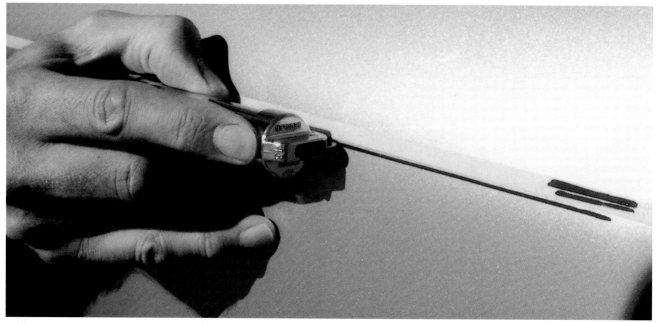

With your guide finger on the tape and the tool parallel to the guide tape, place your pinky finger on the surface. This will keep the wheel head flat.

Here are the most important things to remember:

A Always hold the tool parallel to the tape. If you don't, it's like having your steering wheel on a car turned around when you want it to go straight. The wheel will "walk" or "slide" on you.

B Your thumb and guide finger need to be positioned about 2 inches back from the wheel. The further up your guide finger is, the more the back area of the tool will wobble around. As you move your guide finger back you will notice how much more stable the tool becomes — like a train on a track.

C With your grip on the tool, your guide finger on the tape, and the tool parallel to the guide tape, extend your pinky finger onto the surface so the finger and your thumb act like a set of "training wheels". This will keep the wheel head flat on the surface.

D When pulling the line, notice how the tape feels against your thumb. I like to lightly run my thumbnail on the edge of the tape.

E When pulling the second line, gradually get wider until you reach the desired taper between lines, then lock your hand in that position. This takes practice. You will discover how locking the back of the barrel against your palm is very important in this step. For an open-ended stripe, place a piece of tape vertically across where you want the lines to start or end. When creating double lines, you can use the same-size line, two different sizes, or even two different colors. ∽

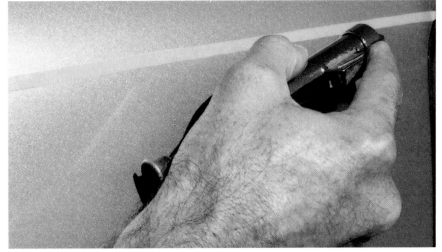

Never hold the tool diagonally.

Use your thumb to help guide you when pulling the line.

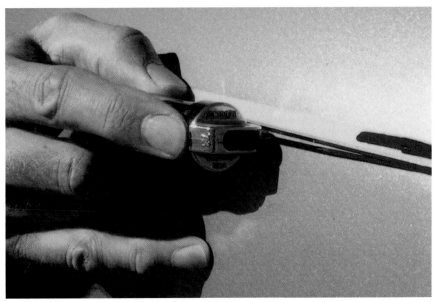

When pulling the second line, gradually get wider until you reach the desired width between lines. Try to lock in your hand in that position as you move along.

Chapter Five

Designs – Simple To Complicated

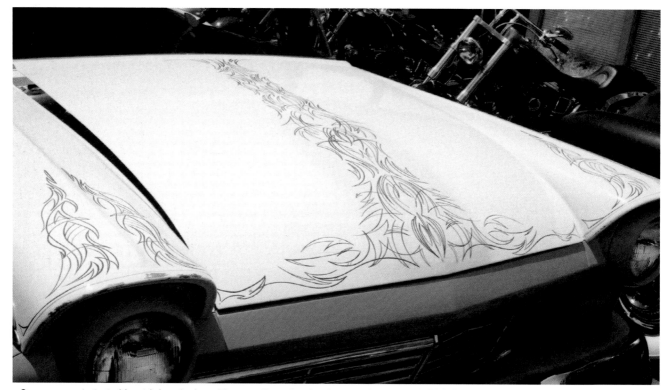

Once you get started in striping designs it's sometimes hard to know when to stop. This is an example of "over-the-top" striping.

After a few months of hanging out with me, my old girlfriends used to be able to spot my work when they saw it. It's funny how sometimes the artist might not be able to identify their work, but other people can. When you first start out you will likely be constantly observing the other guys' work to understand the way they put a design together. You may try to emulate someone else's style until you finally find your own. It might take months, or it might take years.

Picasso said, "good artists borrow, great artist steal." This is what you will be doing for some time after you learn to get the line right. In all good pinstripe designs, the consistency and the size of the line are what dictate the quality of the work. Fine line designs are most impressive. I know a striper in the Northeast whose lines are so fine it looks like he put the design together using threads.

When pinstripers get together for a weekend "Panel Jam," they will often work off each other to come up with designs on wood, plastic or metal substrates. These panels often turn out beautifully. They are truly works of art. For the novice striper, this type of gathering is very helpful. The veteran stripers are seemingly always willing to help the rookie. It's like having many teachers with one student between them.

Each striper has his or her own recipe for a good design. The good stripers can take a bunch of twists and turns that somehow make it all look right. I will attempt to give you some sort of rules of design later, but it's the lines themselves that form a good design.

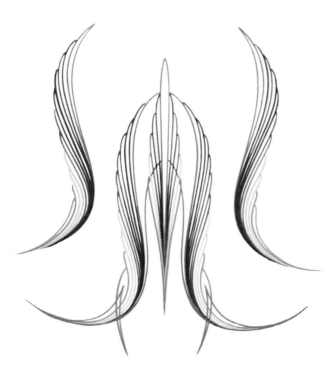

The "feather" is a design frequently used for enhancing door handles, side lights and rear pillar/post areas. The design itself was developed by Lyle Fisk of San Diego.

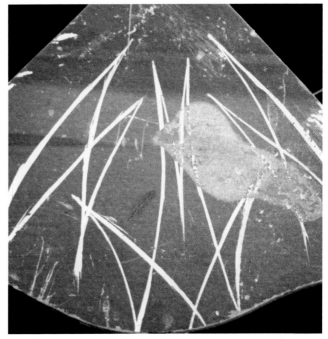

Pinstriping design takes time to learn. Practice, practice, practice. You might not be very good at it in the beginning. I tried to do this Von Dutch-style design when I was 12.

Turn, Turn, Turn

The thickness of the paint is what will help you or mess you up when you turn a striping brush. The paint for turning must be a little thicker than the paint you would use to do a long line. When turned, the brush acts like the rudder of a ship.

One of the easier tasks a striper faces is outlining flames and graphic designs used in custom painting. When I first started hands-on striping workshops, most of my students were custom painters and airbrushers. When you're following an edge it's easier than getting out in the middle of a hood or trunk lid and going for it. Some of this work involves painting on top of the surface, not under the clear coat, and you will need to have a thicker paint just to cover the edge of the work being outlined.

So how do you make the paint thicker, especially when you're also doing the straight line work within the same job? I always have an area of my palette that has wetter paint. You simply load your brush from the area that has dryer paint in it. Take the normal load of paint you get from your cup or bottle of paint and instead of paletting the brush in a wet or clean area of the palette, you simply palette the brush load in an existing area that has been drying for 5-10 minutes. The paint becomes thicker immediately.

Putting together a design is somewhat like reading

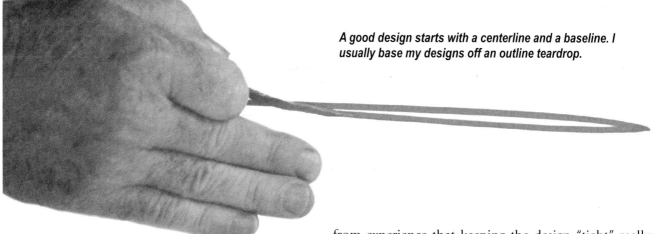

A good design starts with a centerline and a baseline. I usually base my designs off an outline teardrop.

the book of Deuteronomy in *The Bible.* This one begot this one, which begot this one, and so on. This is how the evolution of a pinstriping design works.

The first thing you should do in formulating a design is establish a centerline, base line and perhaps even a grid pattern in Stabillo pencil. The design works off the centerlines, whether it be a teardrop line, that I commonly use, or any other configuration. I've found from experience that keeping the design "tight" really helps. Line designs really look a lot better when they're kept relatively close to each other, so I keep the design tight at the top and gradually work out to the sides.

Let's blow apart a simple design. Notice the elements shown here. Many of your designs will incorporate these lines. The accompanying photos show what they look like all joined together, and what they look like joined together with the teardrop in the middle. The approach is simple, yet very effective.

The elements of the design are on the left, and the assembled elements are on the right.

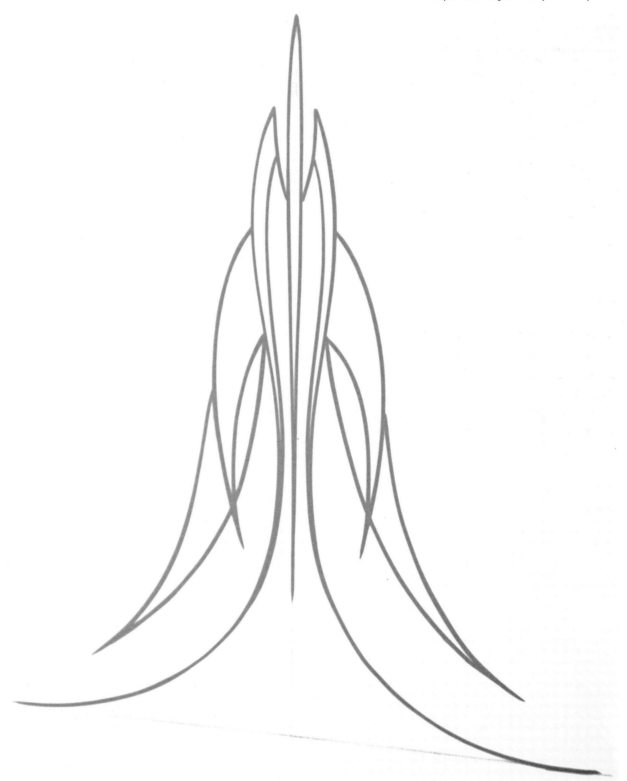

It's usually best to mirror the design from side to side. Perfecting this takes a lot of practice.

Depending on how creative you are, you might want to do the same design on the front and the back of the vehicle with slight variations. Keep in mind that "less is more." Big, complicated designs are great as long as they fit in with your project. As in the lead photo of this chapter, complicated designs are a quagmire of problems. If you're not careful or too inexperienced in putting a piece of work like this together, a complicated design can really get away from you. But if you feel up to it, go for it. If you're not up to it, what the heck, go for it anyway. Experience is the best teacher. Just don't do it on someone's nice car; that is what practice glass is for.

Drawing Out Your Designs

Lately I have been drawing my designs out with Stabillo pencil first for both me and my customers to look at. I started getting in the habit of drawing things out while working in Germany, Switzerland and France starting in the late-1990s. You had to draw out the design for the customer there because, even if they had seen some of these designs in the American car magazines, they still had no real clue what you were about to put on their car. So I started to draw the designs out and found out that I liked seeing what my idea was first before I ever put it on the car (or whatever).

This method does not work on primer or any surface that is rough. The pencil marks will **not** come off. This is especially true of the "paint" on rat rods and customs. You must also be careful not to stripe a car that has too much "dry spray" on the vehicle. Because of the sandpaper-like surface condition of the paint, it will allow the pinstriping paint, no matter whether it's 1 Shot or House of Kolor, to "crawl" and spread away from the edge of the line. It's not a very good look.

Draw in the design using the grid to get an exact mirror image from side to side.

Something a Little Different

Trying to come up with new striping ideas in this day and age can be discouraging, but I was able to push on and come up with my own thick-and-thin style. It's based on the feather and the same center design we just constructed. Instead of the lines being all the same thickness, they are heavier in some areas and thin in others.

The thick-to-thin designs were developed from my observations of the art noveau styles from France. Mucca is one of my favorite poster artists and it is his art that inspired this differentiation of design.

First, draw out a simple grid pattern. This allows you to plan out the design and check for deviation of the mirror image. Next, draw out the design itself, working out the actual elements. Once you're satisfied, start the painting process.

Draw out a grid pattern using a water-based pencil. This will allow you to wipe away the lines after you're finished with the design.

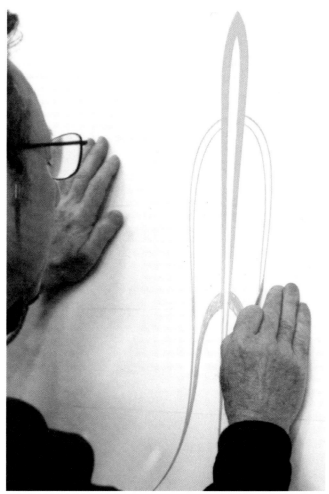

Paint in the outline of the design in each color, then fill everything in.

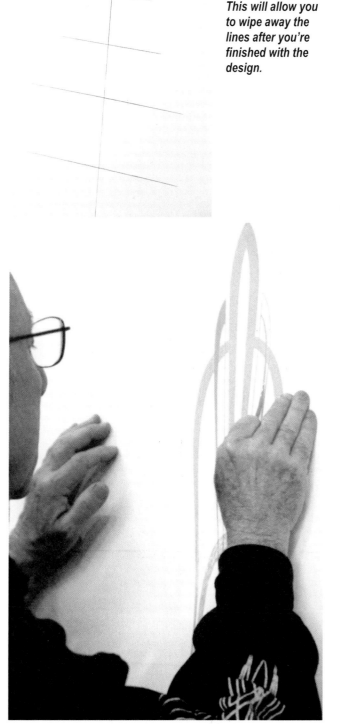

Go to the second color and repeat the process.

Starting from the left side, I paint in the outlines of the design. I work from left to right because I am righthanded, therefore I see the left side of the design best. It's easier to mirror the lines if you can see them. Mirroring takes practice — lots and lots of practice. Once you get your eye-hand control sharper through repetition, it gets easier. Once you have the outlines done, just fill in the centers with your striping brush. You can turn it sideways or even upside down to make the fill in faster. Practice will tell you how to do it.

Next, start your second color, being careful to not get into the wet paint from the first color. You can stop at this point or keep adding more color and lines. My greatest mentor, Cary Greenwood, taught me that it's best to have a design taper down from narrow at the top to wider at the bottom. Most of the designs I create follow this formula.

Make sure you practice doing your designs, whatever style they may be, on a piece of tempered glass or safety plate first. If you eventually need to re-use the glass you can come back with a razor blade and easily scrape off the dried paint.

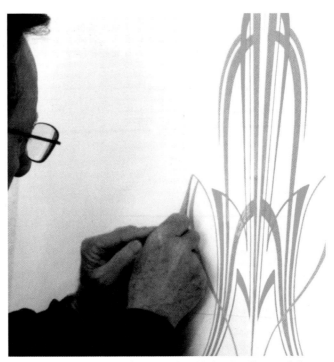

Here I'm outlining and filling in the third color. Be careful that you don't run across any wet paint while crossing over other lines. This is where a good two-handed method really comes in handy.

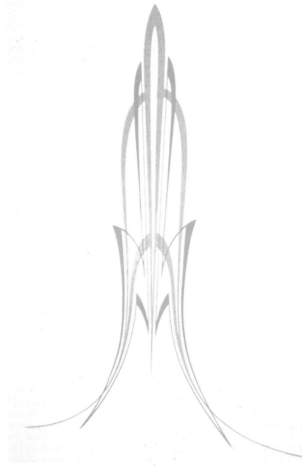

Here's what it looks like after the first two colors are finished. You can leave the design the way it is or keep building it.

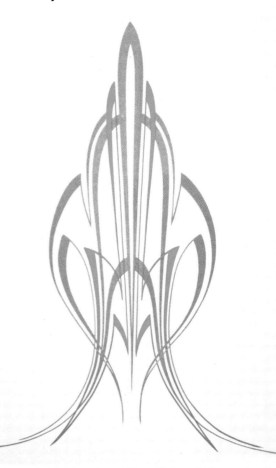

Here's the finished product. Wipe off the grid lines after the paint dries with a soft towel dampened with rubbing alcohol. Don't rub very hard or the new paint might come off.

Reversed Pinstriping Designs

I saw a street rod last year at a big show in Pleasanton, California, that had striping done in pearl over bright candy lime green with pearl. I stopped the owner of the car in mid-cruise and asked him who did the striping on the car. He laughed and said the painter did the striping, but that it was done with tape. I asked him what he meant and he told me that they had taped out all of the striping bodylines and designs in 1/8-inch fine line tape over the base coat of pearl. Then they shot candy lime green over that and pulled off the tape prior to final clearing. The result was a perfectly even line buried in the clear.

Use 1/8-inch 3M fine line plastic tape. Cut off the corners with a sharp razor knife.

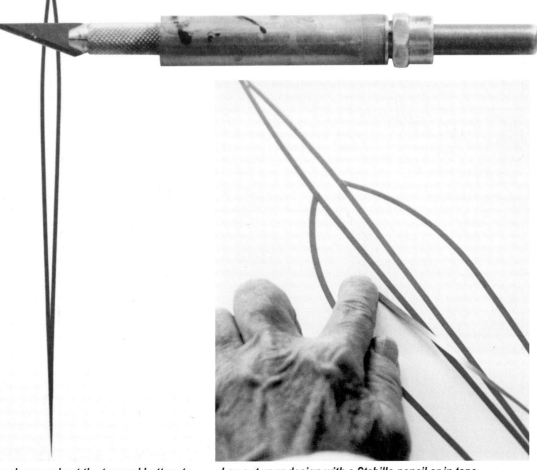

First, lay out a teardrop shape and cut the top and bottom to a sharp point.

Lay out your design with a Stabillo pencil or in tape.

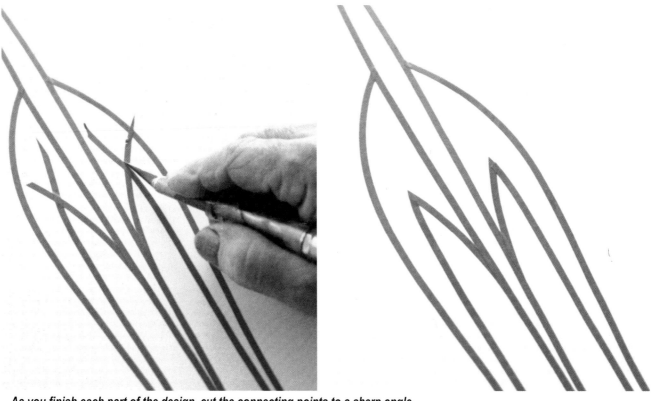

As you finish each part of the design, cut the connecting points to a sharp angle.

When you have finished the design to your satisfaction, use a Scotchbrite pad to rough up the surface prior to paint. Be sure to blow off the area and use a tack rag over the surface before applying the color.

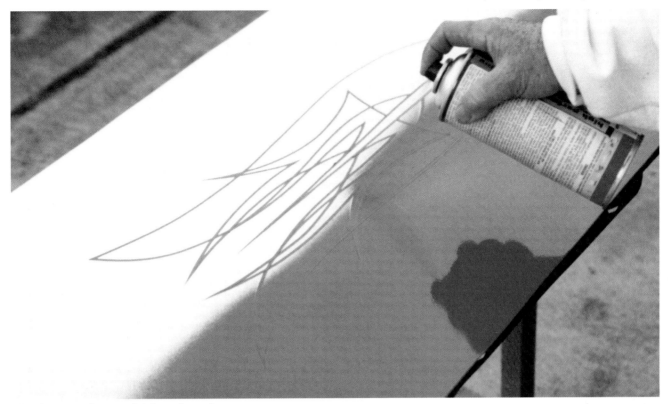

Apply your color completely and evenly.

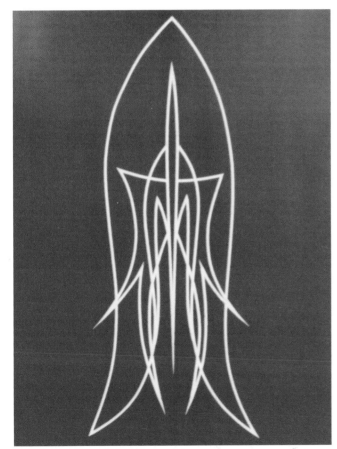

You can have a multi-colored stripe by painting the panel with colors first, then taping off the design and spraying one solid color over the tape. Remove the tape carefully and then cover the design with clear.

Here's how it works. If you're going to do this on a vehicle or just a panel like I'm doing here, you'll need a roll of 1/8-inch 3M fine line tape, a razor knife with a new blade and some patience. Draw a vertical centerline and lay out a teardrop shape. Using the knife, carefully cut the top and bottom of the teardrop to a point. You can lay out your design with a Stabillo pencil first to see what it will look like, or lay out the design with tape only. As you finish each part of the design, use your knife to cut pointed corners at each of the line ends.

Once you have your tape design laid out completely, take a Scotchbrite pad and rough up the surface so the paint will have something to stick to. If you do this on a vehicle that you will be painting over, have the base coat cleared over with inter-coat clear and color sand the surface prior to taping. Now your are ready for paint.

Spray as many coats as needed over the tape until the background is covered. If you want to add more color effects, spray multiple colors around the area where your tape design will be and then cover the colors with tape. Spray a single color over the panel. When you remove the tape you'll have a multi-colored pinstripe with a one-color background.

It's Greek To Me

I've already made mention a couple times of Tommy the Greek teardrops. These were designs that were formed in the late 1920s and resembled water drops moving on the surface from the wind blowing them away. The story goes that after Tommy the Greek washed his car one day and drove it back to the shop, he noticed that the water had formed, what looked like a teardrops, from the wind blowing it, and he designed teardrops from there. Whatever happened, he left us with a style that will be used for many years to come.

Von Dutch was the inventor of modern pinstriping, but the man he admired was Tommy the Greek. Tommy's last name was Hrones, and you don't get much more Greek than that. His style of striping and scallops were synonymous with the San Francisco Bay Area custom car and hot rod scene. He invented his style back in the late 1920s, and let it grow to epic proportions by the 1950s and '60s. You weren't nuthin' if you didn't have Tommy's work on your car, or at least that's what all the locals say. Since Tommy was the first professional striper I really had contact with, my practice style changed from Von Dutch to Tommy the Greek very quickly.

Teardrops are pretty easy to do and very quick to apply. A full set will take just a few minutes to finish. I use Tommy's style as one of the many that I offer my customers. I'm rather conservative about changing the location of the designs, and I also don't like adding to the designs. I figure Tommy had it right to begin with. However with modern cars and trucks, you have to change a little with the style of the body. After all, the look of the scallops and teardrops are for accenting the lines of the cars, not for showing off the artwork. The beauty of his scallops, for instance, was that you could create a sort of bodyline look to a car that had no bodyline. A case in point is the 1955 Chevrolet. You could put his scallops high on a fender or quarter panel and define the bodyline.

First let's start with a set of seven teardrops. This configuration could be used on the front or back of the vehicle on a trunk lid or hood. First make a single teardrop about 4 inches long. I usually use a Mack #2 Series 10 brush. Simply pull a straight line 4 inches down. Then put the tip of the brush at the top of the line and move the brush slightly to the left. Then, while

This collage of different designs originated by Tommy the Greek shows the diversity of his work. Teardrops, scallops, and 1/4-inch lines were his hallmarks. Many stripers have since copied or expounded upon these designs.

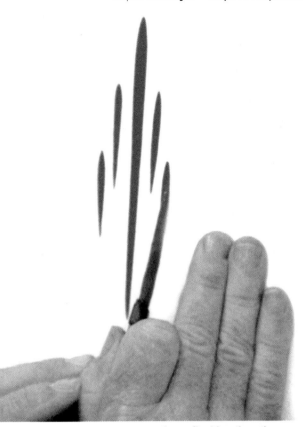

This is the start of a seven-teardrop set. Start with a solid teardrop 4 inches long. Next, put two teardrops flanking the center, one on each side about 2 1/2 inches long.

Move down and do two more teardrops flanking the others.

Add two more flanking the first two sets at the bottom of the center teardrop.

Outline each teardrop with a contrasting color. Use a 1/16-inch line or finer to do the outline. Tommy never outlined his work with a very broad line.

moving it down, turn the brush inward toward the center and gradually move it towards the center to the bottom of the line. Do the same thing on the opposite side of the teardrop right to left to the bottom. This will give you the basic shape of a large teardrop.

Next, put flanking teardrops flanking the large one — one on the right, one on the left. These teardrops are formed by putting the brush at the top of where the teardrop will go in each position. Pull the brush slightly out to the left and then gently back to center. Do the same but in reverse on the opposite side. Move down and do two more teardrops flanking the others, but lower. At this point you should have a seven-teardrop set ready to be outlined.

Start outlining the teardrops as shown in the accompanying photos. Tommy never outlined his work very broadly. He always used fine lines. About 1/32 inch will do. The accompanying photos some design layouts that I have seen used in various places around a car. The "scallop" designs could be used over a grille area or a to accent the bottom of a truck lid. The "half lance" head and was used by Tommy to start a line at the beginning of a fender or quarter panel. All of these designs should be outlined with a 1/32-inch line. The traditional colors used were white, black or red. However, I have seen other colors used, especially in modern days, or if a customer has his own ideas.

This 1968 Mustang has classic Tommy the Greek-style striping.

Panel Art

When I first started teaching pinstriping in 1997 I was faced with the daunting task of trying to explain to my students what a pinstriping design is and where to get some ideas of what a good design look like. I was in Germany at the time, and there weren't very many good examples around. Since then I have picked up a lot of ideas from all over the world through sign and custom paint trade magazines, and in recent years, the Internet has made it much easier to find information about designs.

Panel art has evolved a lot since the early 1980s. I think it was started by pinstripers that used to come to the "Rat Fink" reunions hosted by Ed "Big Daddy" Roth. They were held at various locations around the country. These get-togethers spawned a new type of painting party called panel jams. Nowadays, you can find these at most of the big indoor car shows around the U.S. Following are some examples of panel art by some of the best in the world:

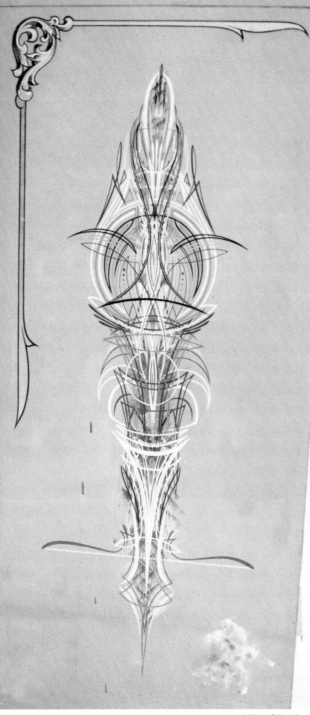

Although it isn't a panel, this storage cabinet at Mike Cline's shop in Sacramento is a fine example of artwork done for the sake of the art itself.

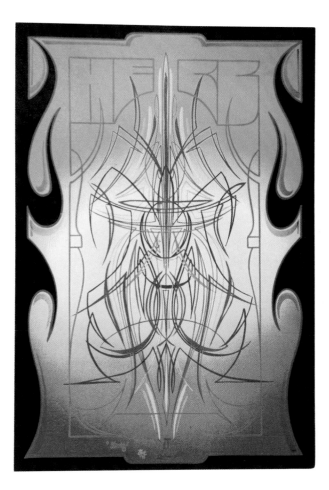

This group effort panel was done at Lead East in 1995 by Glen Design, Howie Nisgor, David Hightower, Julian "Mr. J" Braet, Nick and the author. The finish outlining flames, brushes and name were done by Howie Nisgor.

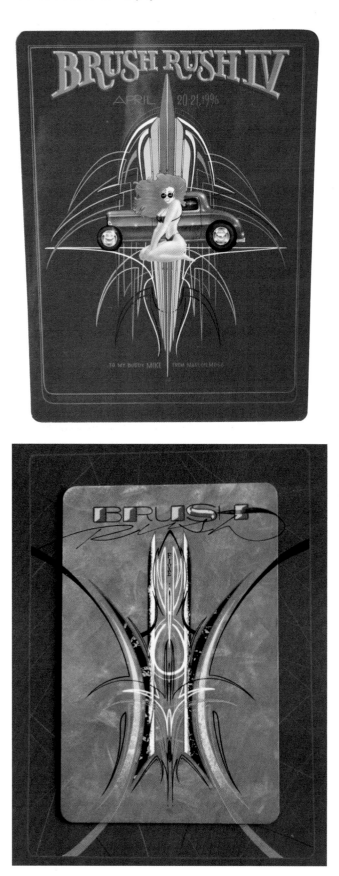

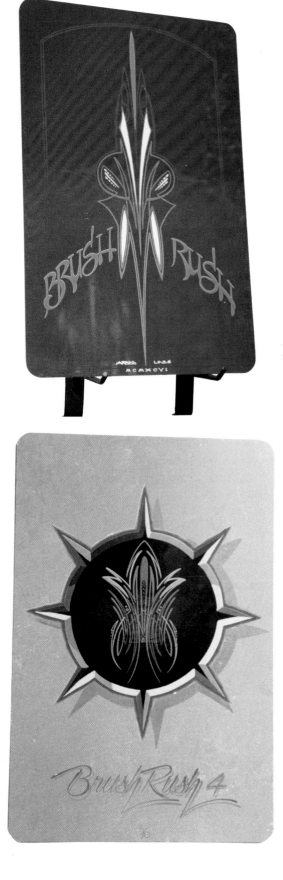

These panels were done for "The Brush Rush" in Sacramento in 1995 and 1996. Top left: Marlon Moss; top right: Ron Ballew; bottom row: two unknowns.

Paul Martin

Marlon Moss

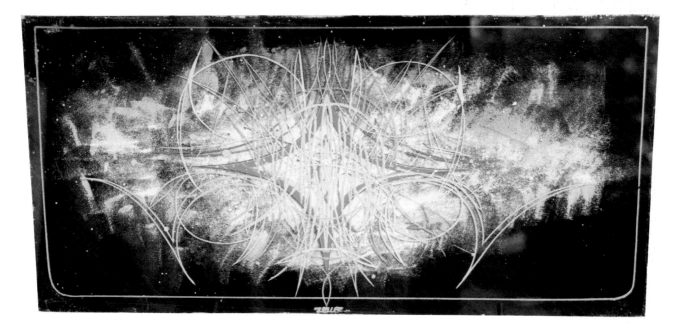

Howard Zeller

Harry Malicoat

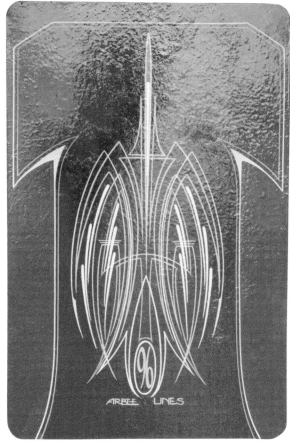

Ron Ballew

Ron Ballew

The art of pinstripe designs came right out of the old days when Von Dutch started covering up grinder marks. These designs got better and better as the years went on. In my travels around the U.S. and the world I have been able to capture on film some really great

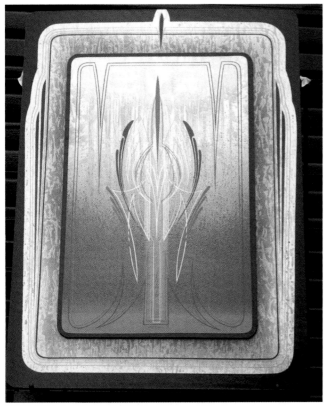

Ron Ballew

designs from some of the best stripers ever seen. This portfolio is meant to show of their work.

I'll start with a few distinct styles that haven't seen much exposure. Stripers have all sorts of styles, and many are quite different from each other. Some stripers have influenced entire regions like the central California area around Fresno. Some of the best and most innovative fine line men came from this area.

The Fresno Style

Neil Averill is credited for starting the quarter line/fine line style in the 1960s. He was heavily influenced by Tommy the Greek and his quarter lines. Like Tommy, Neil did teardrops, but his were different. They were very small and shaped quite differently then Tommy's. Once Averill got tired of just doing quarter lines, he added a tiny accent line running parallel to the other line and even put hairlines in the center of the quarter line. Next came leaf-like flourishes at the end of the line and at integral parts of the line, and later mini-graphics. The style because quite influential.

The Fresno style involves bending the line in ways that completely redefine an automobile or truck bodyline.

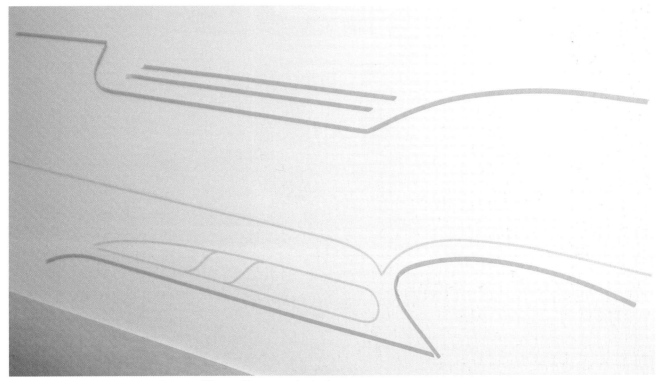

This is the basic tape layout for two different Fresno-style designs.

Fresno style is all about details — many details. From 1/64 to 1/100-inch lines, to the larger more-common sizes, it's the details that make the style work.

The accompanying photos show two layouts done on a 2 x 4-foot aluminum panel. The green tape will be the quarter lines and the 1/8-inch tape will be the finer lines.

Outline the quarter lines with blue fine line 3M tape.

Here's how it should look when you finish taping it up.

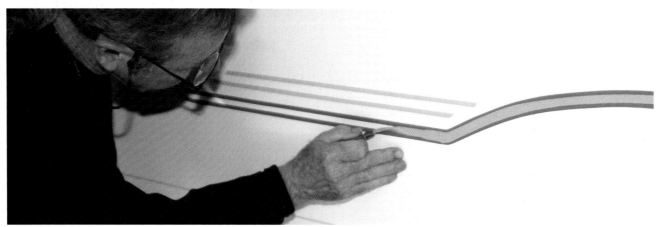

Start painting in the quarter lines. The top one will be lavender and the bottom one light blue.

Outline the quarter lines with 1/4-inch 3M fine line plastic tape. This tape bends well and seals well against bleeding. Fill in in your quarter line with color. In my example, I use one color per line. Other ways you can fill in the line include multi-colored blends, gold leaf, or special effects such as sponge or Saran Wrap.

Outline the quarter lines with a complimentary color about 1/16-inch wide on both side. Next, outline the panels using a color that will compliment the base color and not stand out too much. I use the same rule of thumb as sign painters for applying a drop or cast shadow: Make the color two or three shades lighter or darker than the

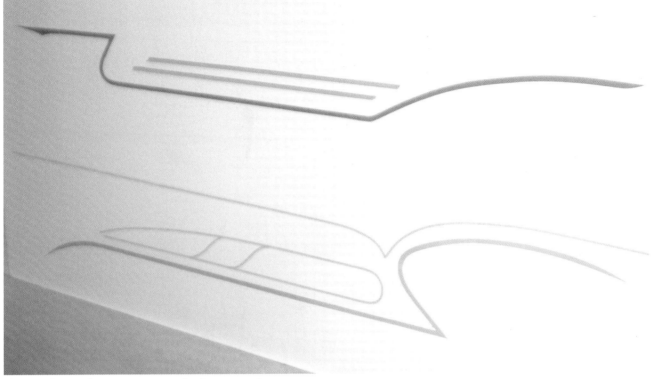

Now we're starting to see some color in our panel.

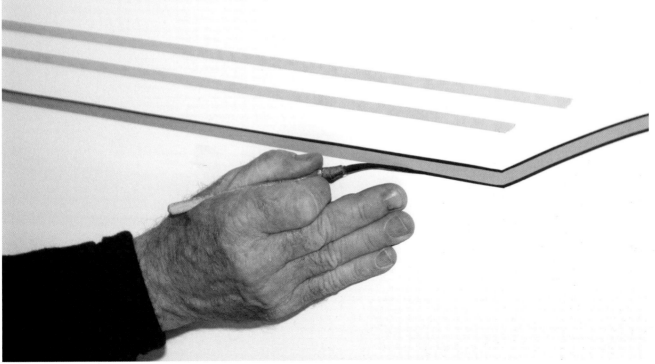

Using a 000 long-handled Mack Series 10 brush, I'm outlining the quarter lines in a darker color.

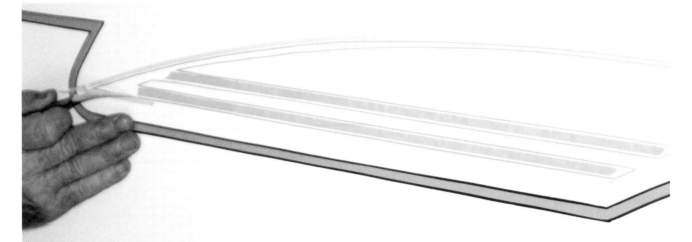

Once I've got the outlines on, I start to paint in the panels light gray. These panels should be half-tones of the base color.

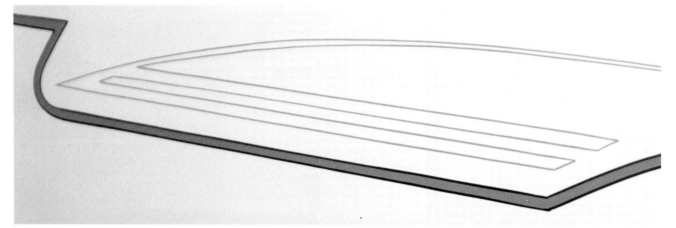

The panels should always compliment the design of the quarter line layout.

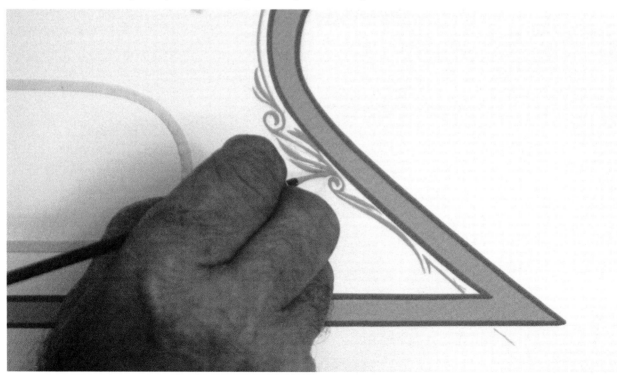

These little scrolls add an accent to the curved areas of the quarter lines. The accent lines themselves are only 1/32-inch wide, and the scrolls should also be as small as the lines. Use a single 0 quill brush for the scrolls.

base color. If it's a dark color stay with darker shadows; if it's a light color stay with lighter complimentary colors.

Little scrolls are used to add detail and compliment parts of the quarter line.

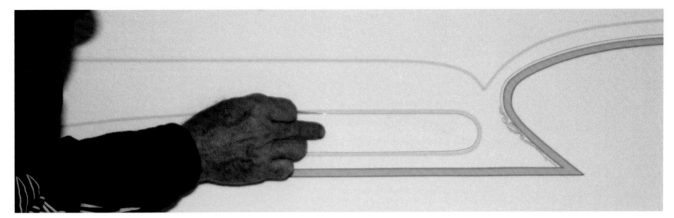

After the scrolls and fine lines are done, I'll paint in the panels.

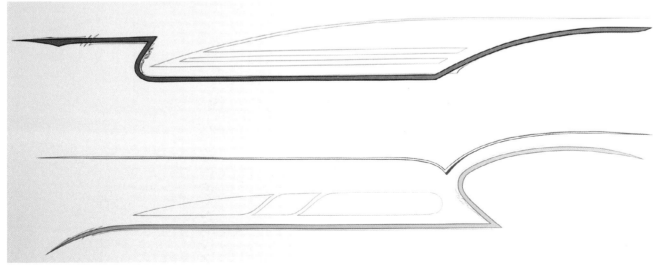

This little line end demonstrates the use of 3M transparent tape as a block-off for the painted line. There are endless possibilities for the fine lines to wander around the quarter line.

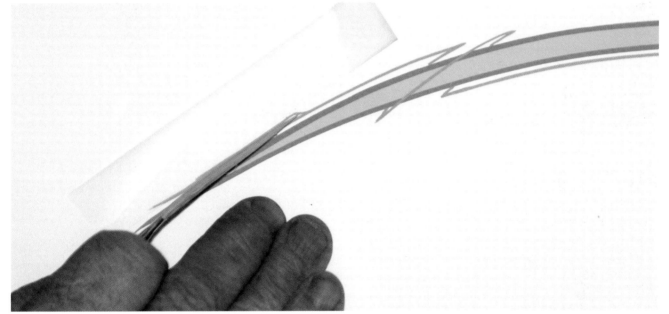

The finished panel shows two distinctly different layouts, both using quarter lines and panels in concert.

A great example of quarter line/panel line designing is this C-5 Corvette striped by Craig Judd from Chowchilla, California.

The Bay City Style

This style incorporates a star or cross for the basis of the design. The Bay City look works well as an accent for wide, open areas on sides and fender tops, panels, deck lids and hoods — any place where there is a wide or long expanse to cover or accent. The style was started at B.A.D. Signs in Redwood City, California, and further developed by Mike Farley. Bay City Vans had them stripe the van with no extra custom paint. The striping covers the whole van and gives it a very distinctive look. The author took over the account from Mike Farley in 1979 and continued the style until 1981. Striping is by Mike Farley and the author.

Here's how it's done:

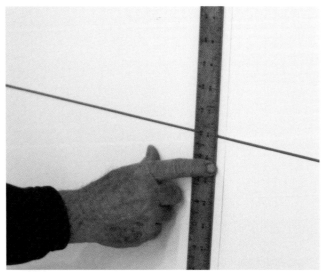

1 *No matter whether it's a panel this size, the whole side of a van or the hood of a car, always measure out the area to be worked within. Start with the star and measure the vertical and horizontal lines, making sure to stop and start the line within 1 1/4 inches of the points of the star.*

2 *I'm using blue line tape here, but normally I would be using 3M 1/8-inch paper tape. Outline your base star design around the tape.*

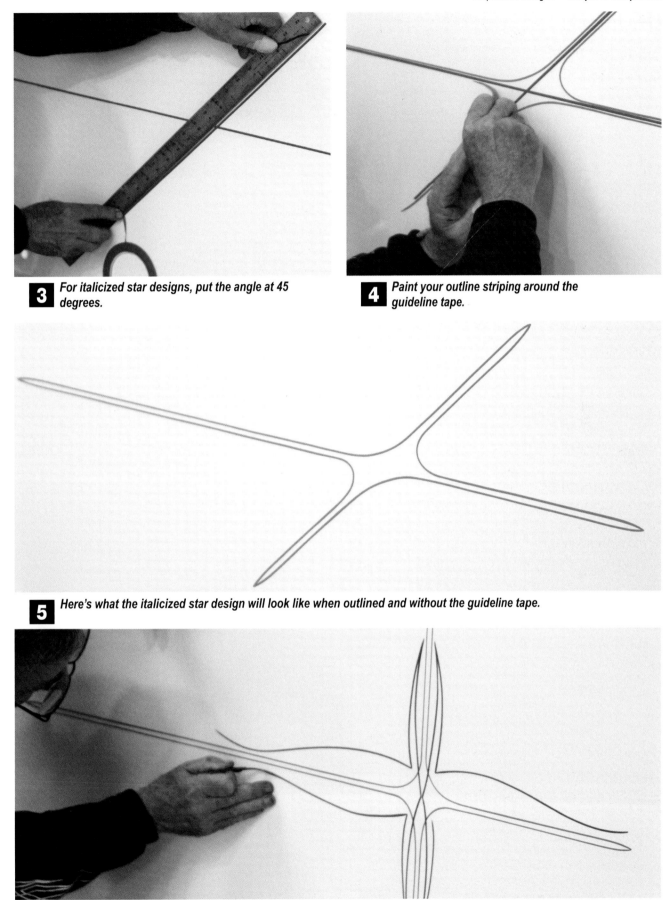

3 *For italicized star designs, put the angle at 45 degrees.*

4 *Paint your outline striping around the guideline tape.*

5 *Here's what the italicized star design will look like when outlined and without the guideline tape.*

6 *Once the basic star design is painted, paint the second color design around the star. These **Designs** should be very simple and mirrored exactly.*

7 *Here I am finishing up the first color. Notice that I have made the design about 2/3 smaller than the star itself. I've found that if you make your design too big it will overpower the basic star design and you'll lose the look you're after.*

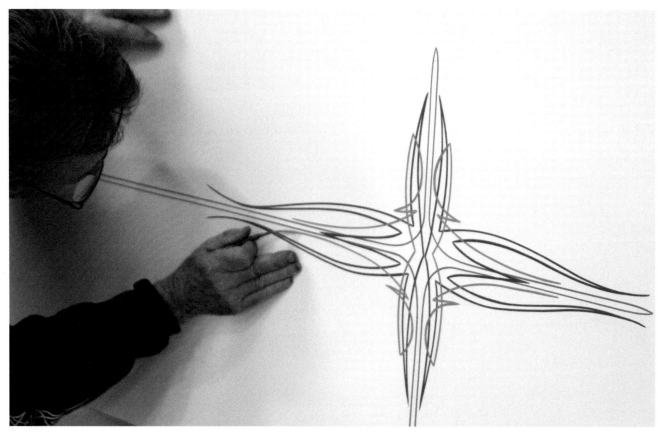

8 *I recommend only using three colors, including the star. Otherwise, the colors confuse the line art and the design looks too busy.*

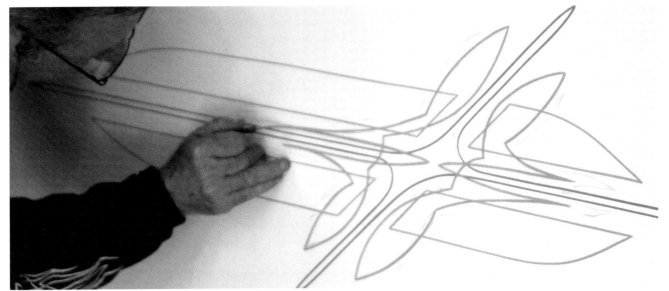

9 *I decided to add some panels flanking all four sides of the star to give the design a little extra flair. I should have left the design this simple.*

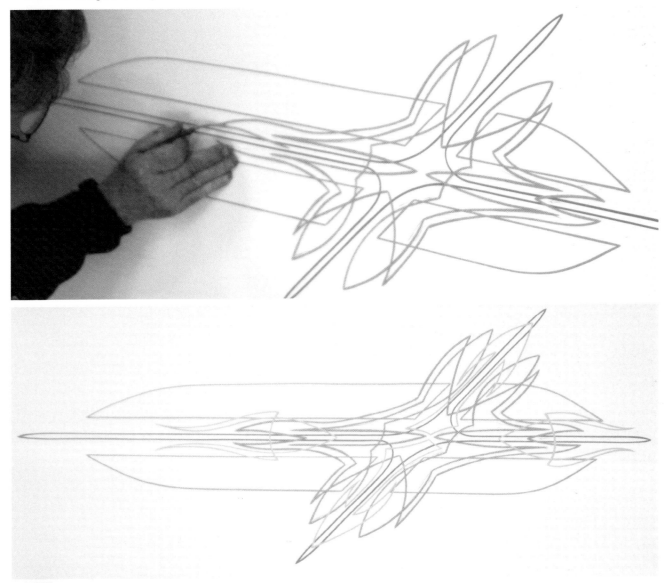

10 *This design is almost too busy for my tastes. Still, as pinstripe art goes, this is a nice design.*

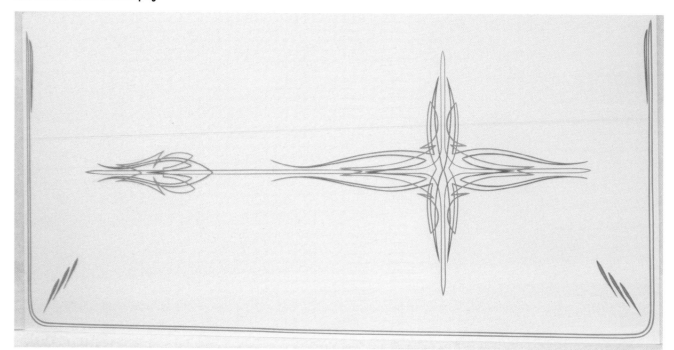

11 *This design is a great example of the Bay City Vans style. It has a center star design and a smaller, simpler design on the end. Teardrops were used judiciously around various points of the van and mixed into the hood and rear door designs. Bodyline pinstriping was also added around the windows, center bodyline, and lower bodylines and a few designs were incorporated into the bodylines themselves.*

Following are a few good examples of layouts from striper Mike Farley.

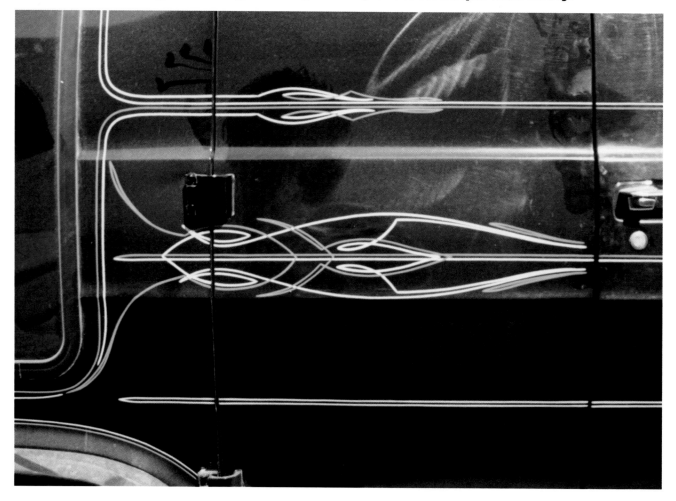

The Bay City Vans style is very distinct and unique.

Classic Designs or "Old School"

Most striping designs include a series of curves, long lines and short lines. Mirror image is the other factor in the design. Following is a look at some "old school" designs that include these traditional elements. Some of these designs are mixed with graphic effects and even murals.

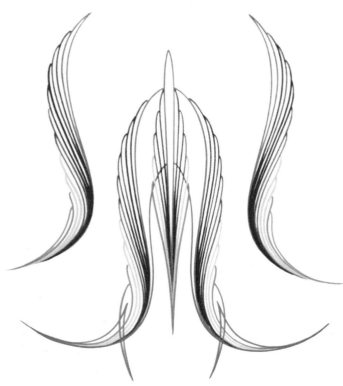

The rainbow design was originally created by Cary Greenwood. (Striping by the author.)

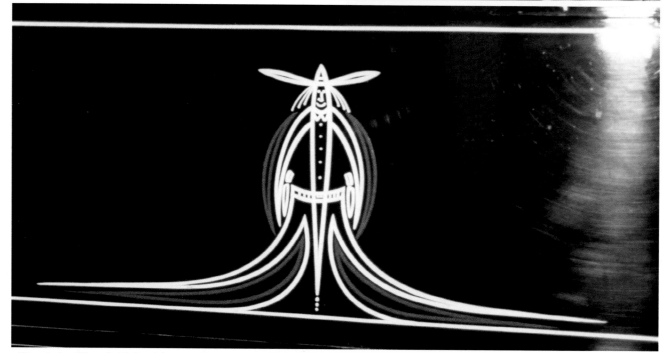

Classic traditional striping (above and top right) by Tom Kelly of Kelly & Son, Bellflower, California.

Striping by cartoon master Dave Bell, Falcon Heights, Minnesota.

This heavily striped 1932 Ford roadster was done in the old classical style of the 1950s. (Striping by Pete "Hot Dog" Finlan, San Diego.)

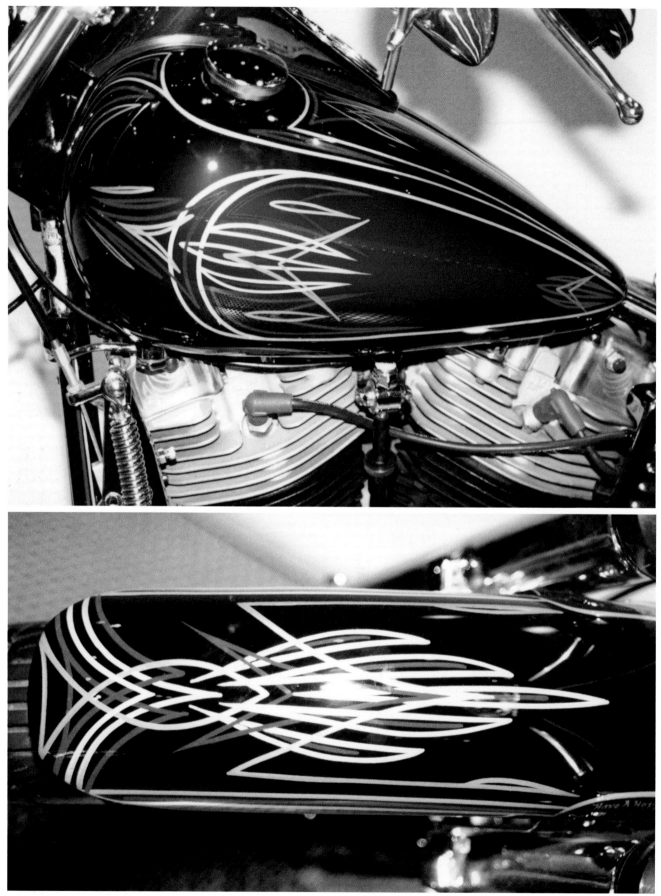

Striping by the inventor of modern pinstriping himself, Von Dutch. This Harley was on display at the Petersen Museum.

Custom painter Art Himsl did this classic deck lid design back in 1961. This is one of the few examples of early striping that is still intact today.

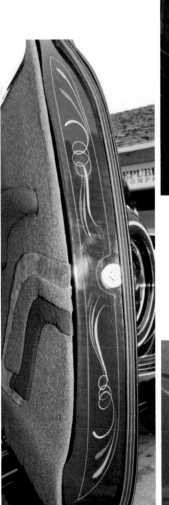

Here are a few more examples of curls getting into the classic and graphic design. Allan Smith of Salinas, California (left) has a way with curls. Below, curls are great accent designs for use in an outline panel. (Pinstriping by author.)

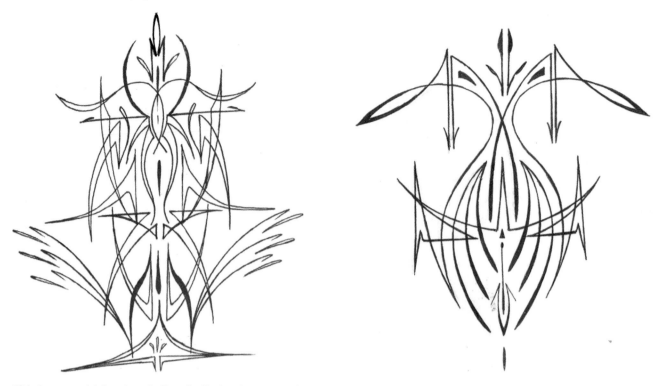

This is some striping done in Russia. Notice that some of the designs look like 1950s-style American striping and some of it looks like old wagon-style or coachwork striping from the early 1900s. A very nice mix. (Pinstriping by Ken Platonov)

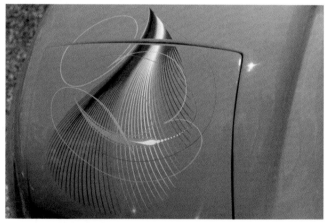

"Alex in Wonderland" is one of the premier striper/artists of our time is know quite well on the East Coast. Like Von Dutch, he is known for both his antics and his striping mastery.

Here are some classic deck lid designs. What a diversity of line and design.

Signing Your Work

I'm always disappointed I can't find a name on someone's beautiful work. There are many ways that pinstripers sign their work, but all state-of-the-art signatures are done very, very small. The artist's should be barely recognizable. Most signatures are so small they like a flaw in the paint. The first signature I ever saw was on a Triumph chopper in the early 1970s painted by Bob Kovacs of Fresno. Under the cartoon and lettering that said "Wild Cherry", there was his signature. It was 1/16 inch high and lettered in both thick and thin script and read "Kovacs." Needless to say, I was highly impressed and started to sign my work in the same way from that point on.

Signatures that small don't photograph well, so I hope you can use your imagination. 〜

Chapter Six

Flames

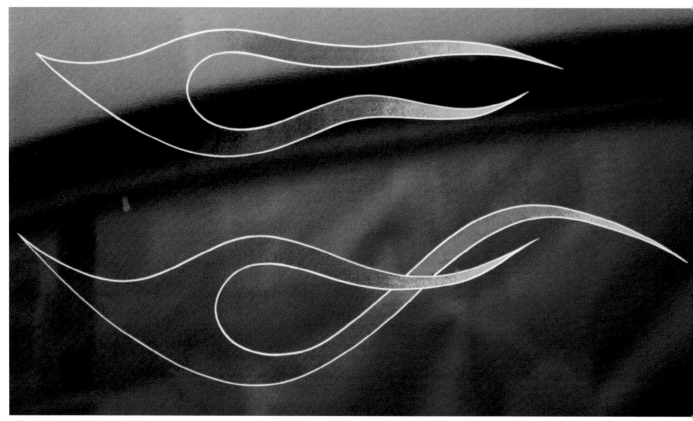

These are crossover and parallel running flames from Real Ralph Newman of Santa Cruz, California. They show two different ways to do sponge multi-color flames.

When you're hot, you're hot, and flames have been hot in custom pinstriping for many years. Outline flames have been with us for a long time. Whether it's outlining custom painted flames or just outlines alone, flames are a mainstay in a striper's bag of tricks. Just outlining flames for custom painters doing full flame jobs will keep you busy if you get good at and have a few connections.

A few years back I saw some outline flames being done by Real Ralph Newman and Jim Bradley. They were having their way with an old Chevy pickup late one night at Hot August Nights in Reno. After laying out the design and taping off the flames, they started using a sea sponge to filling the inside of the flame before they outlined it. I thought, "Wow, what a concept!" I've been doing the same technique ever since.

To get better contrast, use sponge rubber instead of a sea sponge to do color fill work inside the outlines of the flames.

Lay out your flames by crossing over each of the licks, then cut them out before sponging in the color.

Some guys, like Ralph, have refined it a bit and now do "crossover" flames as well as the stock, standard variety. You get the most visibly graphic results using sponge rubber cut into small blocks as seen in the accompanying photos. By taping off the flame and cutting out the crossover, you make it easy to tape off one side of the flame and sponge in the color. But let's not get ahead of ourselves. Following are the stops involved in this flame job, just the way I saw it was done that night.

Mask off the flame that will be under the overlaid flame tip. Remove the mask and carefully sponge one of the other colors in the flame next to the overlaid tip. This adds dimension to the design.

Taping and Pouncing

I suggest that the owner of the vehicle be there to approve any final layout when you're doing flames for somebody else. Don't forget that the basic layout tape is your guideline for your outline flame lines. Once the layout is done, you will probably need to pull a pattern so you can do a mirror image layout on the other side. 3M has a paper that is meant for masking but is an artist's dream. It's semi-transparent, comes in four widths and is relatively cheap compared to using vellum, a pattern paper.

If you are doing a flame job for somebody else, have them approve it before you start laying down lines.

Start by laying down pattern paper over the flame layout and pencil in the inside edge of all the flames.

To paint the PT Cruiser shown in the accompanying photos we used 36-inch wide 3M paper, part #6540. This was too wide, so we cut the width down using an Olfa knife. We cut the paper down to about 24 inches — enough for the pattern we are demonstrating.

When doing your pattern, start with the front work toward the back making sure to get all the lines (flames) on the pattern. I use the inside of the flame as my guide. By taking a sharp pencil and pressing down slightly, you will be able to ride the inside edge of the tape. Be sure to establish some "indexing marks" on your door edges, bodylines, or wherever — you want to get the pattern back in the same spot on the opposite side of the car. Since the paper is semi-transparent you will need to make the index marks darker by going over them with a marker or "Sharpie" pen. This will show through when the pattern is turned over to the opposite side of the paper.

Next, we remove the pattern from the vehicle and bring it to an area where you can "pounce" — meaning to put perforated holes into the paper for transferring the flame pattern. You need a wide-open area, free of

Using a "pounce wheel," perforate or "pounce" the holes into the pattern paper.

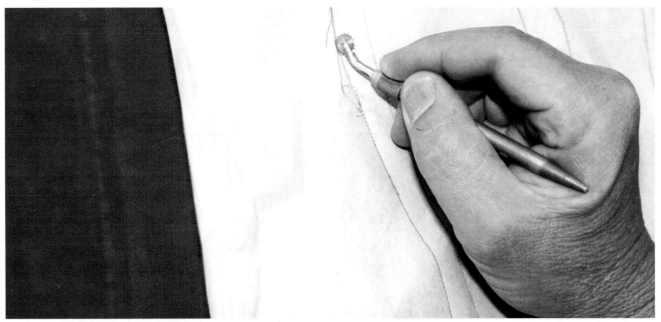

I use a synthetic velvet cloth under the pattern. You don't need to push down on the tool as hard if you use this method.

Bring the pattern to the opposite side of the vehicle and tape it up securely. Make sure all your indexing marks are lined up with the pattern.

obstructions. The last thing you want around a pattern is an object in the way that could tear the paper. I always put a felt or, in this case, synthetic velvet cloth under the pattern. This helps the pounce wheel glide through the paper effortlessly and doesn't wear out your wrist by forcing you to push down hard on the pattern to make your holes.

Once you've finished pouncing the pattern, put it onto the opposite side of the car. Be careful to match all your indexing points. At this point you'll need a pounce bag. This is a homemade tool used for patting chalk or baby powder on the surface. You can make it from a shop rag filled with either baby powder for white powder or lamp black chalk (available through

To make a pounce bag, first fill it full of marking chalk in the middle of the rag.

Fold all of the corners up together and secure them.

This folded and loaded pounce bag is ready for use. Pat the bag lightly on the surface to "prime" the chalk through the material.

sign supply companies). Pour a pile about 2 inches high. Then join all four corners of the rag together. Take a rubber band and wrap the rag as shown. That's all there is to it.

Take your pounce bag and rub it gently on the surface of the paper, occasionally patting it on the surface to release a little more chalk dust. Rub it a little more, pat it, then rub a little more. You want to try to get just the right amount of chalk dust on the vehicle. After completing this step, lift the pattern and get it out of the way.

The next step is to draw in the pounce pattern lines in Stabillo

Rub the bag over the pattern holes, tapping the bag occasionally to get more powder out. You should hold down the pattern in uneven areas to allow the paper to be flat to the surface so the pattern transfers correctly.

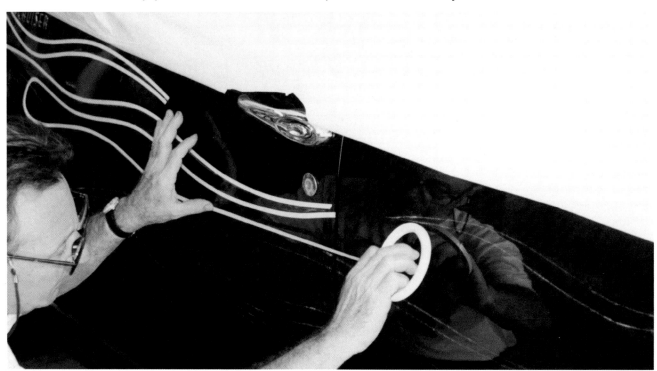

Once you're done pouncing, lift the bottom of the pattern up and tape it to the vehicle. Don't remove the pattern yet, you might need to drop it down later. At this point you can start taping the outline of all the flames.

pencil. This is a very important step. You don't want to lose your lines or you'll be starting the process all over again. Keep that in mind if you decide to skip drawing in the lines and just apply the tape. After you've drawn in the lines, begin laying down the tape. Make sure to take your time.

After you tape up all the flames, remove the pattern and start to tape the edges with 3M Blue Line tape. Make sure to mash the Blue Line edges down with your fingernail to prevent bleeding underneath the tape.

Once you have your basic layout tape down, start laying down your blue fine line tape for a sponge painting barrier. I usually add another layer of tape outside the flame layout. This keeps paint away from the outer edge of the flame when you are doing your sponge work. It's easy to forget and get the paint outside the layout — then you have a messy cleanup afterwards. (Yeah, I know, I didn't do that here, but it's still a good idea).

Sponge Painting Inside The Flames

Now you're ready to start painting. Start with some small pieces of sea sponge. It's easier to get an even blend of colors with smaller pieces. Wet the sponge and dry it off until it is only slightly damp. A wet sponge is softer than a dry one and easier to work with.

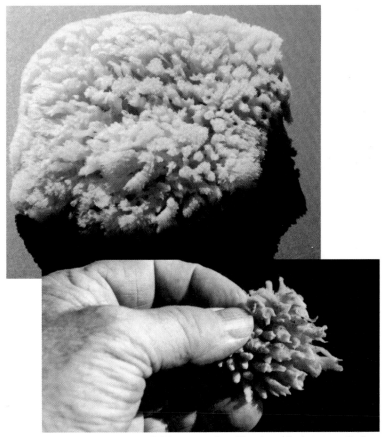

Sea sponges are available at your local hardware/paint store. Pull a small piece out of the sponge for use with each color.

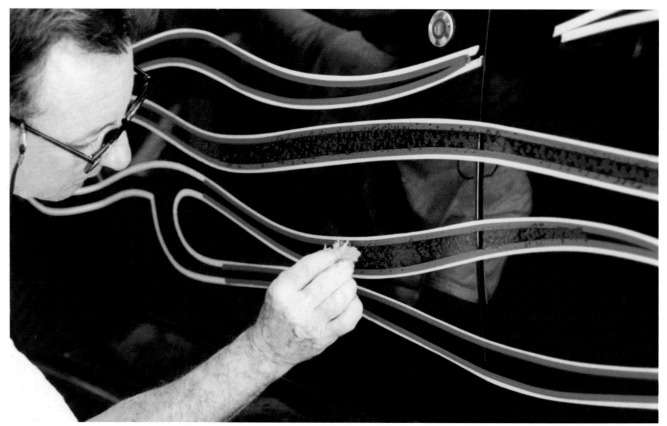

Start sponging with the darker color first. Use the sponge like you would an airbrush if you were making a blend, gradually fading out the color.

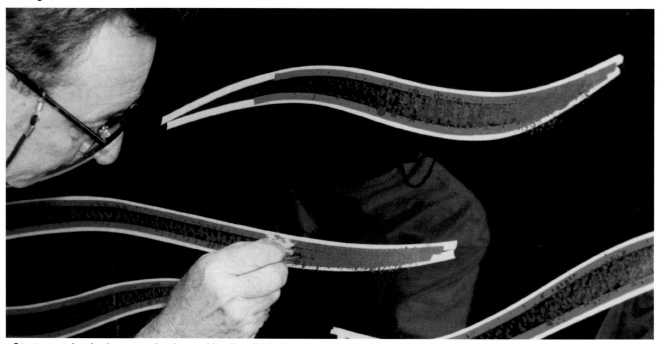

Start sponging in the second color, making it solid in the tips and then fading it into the darker color.

Start with a darker color first. I usually pour a little spot of color out on my palette, about 4 inches in diameter. Dab the sponge into the paint to load it up. Once it's loaded, dab the color onto the palette again, working off some of the excess paint. Excess paint will only run down the side of the car and spoil the look of the sponge effect. After you have carefully laid down all the darker color, load up another chunk of sponge and do your lighter color (if you want one). On this project we used a lighter color on the tips of the flame. Blend

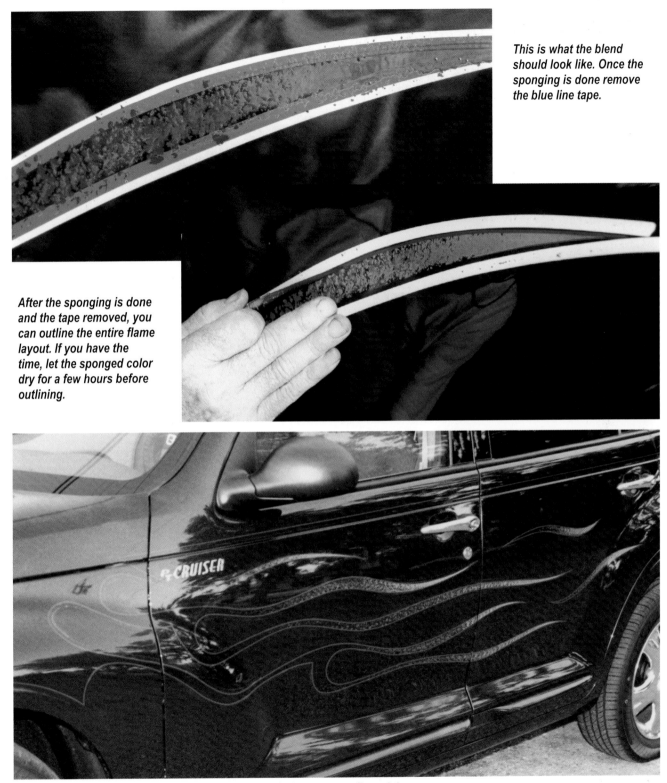

This is what the blend should look like. Once the sponging is done remove the blue line tape.

After the sponging is done and the tape removed, you can outline the entire flame layout. If you have the time, let the sponged color dry for a few hours before outlining.

After outlining the layout, pull up all the tape and admire your new flame job.

the colors as well as you can. Step back frequently to check if the colors are blending evenly. If you get a little overboard with the lighter color, you can always go back and add some more of the darker color.

Once you've finished blending, you're ready to pull off the barrier and blue tape and outline your flames.

If you don't have a time constraint, let the flame blends dry overnight. If your sponge paint is dry, you don't have to worry about running your hand over it while you are outline the design.

So there you are — a nice flame job at one-third the price of a custom painted flame job.

Outline Options

A few new types of flames have evolved since I first started doing custom paint and pinstriping in the late 1950s. It's hard to keep up with what's new and what you should think about putting outside of these flame jobs. Case in point: Craig Frasher had problems getting a striper to come outline a flame job just finished for the SEMA Show. So he has to stripe it himself. Craig doesn't know how to stripe, so he wings it. The outlines look like slashes. He calls it "slash striping" and by the end of the SEMA Show, it's a new trend. Who would have known? This story is crazy, but true. It's the way trends start sometimes. Just by a fluke. Slash striping is a really different look compared to the old standard style of laying a line consistently around the flame.

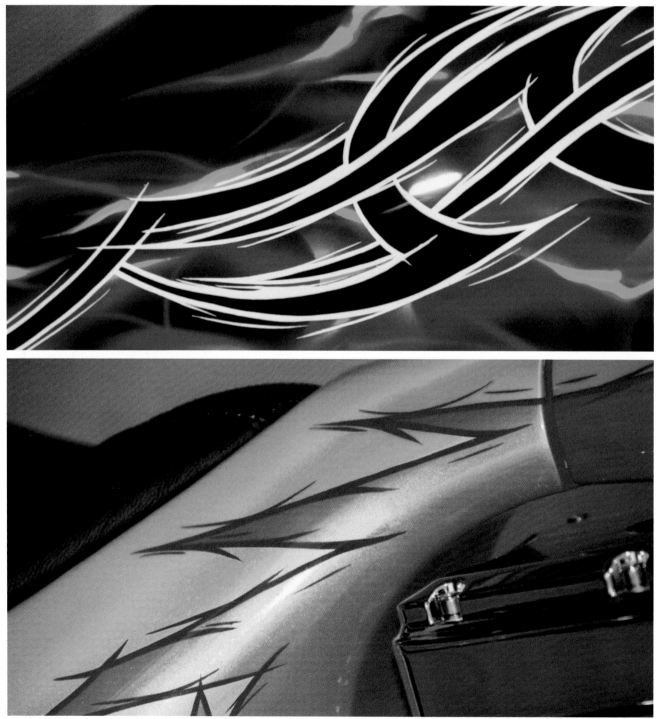

Here are a couple examples of "slash striping." It's a great-looking effect, but very time consuming. You might want to charge extra for this technique if you are doing it for a customer.

So what about the so-called "tribal" flame? Where did this come from? I can only really hazard a guess. I had a conversation with Craig Frasher one day about this subject. He pointed out that his first tribals came from a custom painter/air brusher in the San Francisco Bay Area name Horst. He didn't say when or what year. I know Horst and if Craig says he was first to do it, I would back him up. Horst is a tremendously talented artist who has been painting for some 35 years or more.

"Tribal" flames are another cool approach. I have yet to learn how to lay these bad boys out.

Elongated, snaky, skinny flames are another approach. These flames go well in long, narrow areas that need a little less negative space. I remember a guy named Carl Hovey in San Leandro, California, that did these sorts of "flat flames" at Tony Del Rio's shop. He did them real long and skinny. This was in the mid-1970s. Thirty years later, rod builder Bobby Alloway hired custom painters Wade Hughes and Joshua Shaw to do his flames and paint. These long, slinky flames have now been christened "Ohio flames." Whatever you call them or wherever

This type of layout goes well in a long narrow area. Called Ohio flames, this style was originally done by Bill Roell in North Carolina. These examples are from Wade Hughes and Joshua Shaw.

the layout is indigenous to doesn't really matter. The important thing is to make the customer (or yourself) happy and get more work to do another day.

Below are a couple of examples of outline flames. These designs can have two to four colors. Some use graphice accents in the middle.

Putting one flame layout over another can be a very hot design.

If two colors are good, then three colors are better, at least with this 1948 Ford.

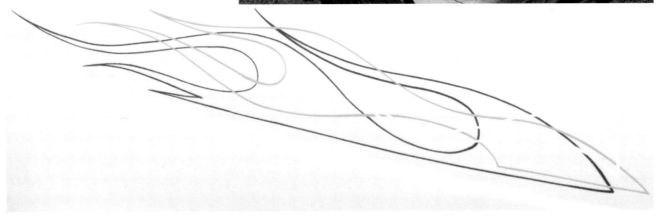

Chapter Seven

The Gold Standard – How To Do Gold Leaf Pinstriping

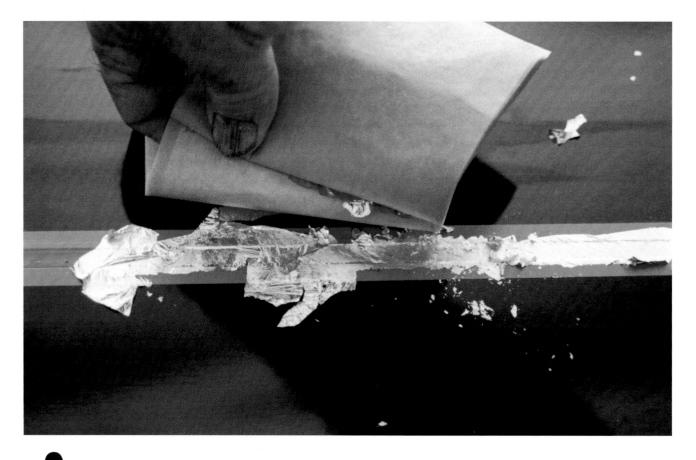

Gold leaf is perhaps one of the most misunderstood forms of pinstriping. Many stripers think it is difficult to do this type of work and don't even consider it. Most customers think it's too expensive because it's "gold." Some think it will make their car look like a fire truck. I'd like to dispel a few of these myths.

Gold leaf is not that hard to do. If you get a kick out of doing artsy-craftsy things, this is your medium. It doesn't have to wear out quickly or require special care, other than the usual wash and wax. A single line of leaf with no outlines is a little harder to do than a line of leaf that's taped off, but with a little practice you'll be on your way. So what's the big deal?

Gold sizing comes in a few varieties of drying time: slow (24 hours) and quick (2 to 4 hours)

House of Kolor Imitation Gold can also be used for sizing with the catalyst. It dries in 10 minutes and can be used under urethane clearcoats.

Whether it's a design or straight line, gold leafing has three steps to consider. The leaf adheres to the vehicle surface using special varnish-type glue called size. Sizing comes in a few varieties according to drying time. There is a slow (24-hour) size and a fast (3- to 4-hour) size. Once you apply the size to the surface, you have only the recommended time to apply your leaf. From there you apply the paint, which is urethane striping enamel. House of Kolor imitation gold (U05) with the catalyst (KU 200) added can be used for size. It only takes about 10 minutes to set and then you can start to guild. HOK clear for striping (UC 3) with a catalyst can also be used. UC 3 is an acrylic urethane. Add a little imitation gold to it for color. It only takes a few minutes longer if you use this formula. A water-based adhesive is also available. Some painters feel this adhesive is more compatible with urethane clears and will use it for gilding gold for under-clear work.

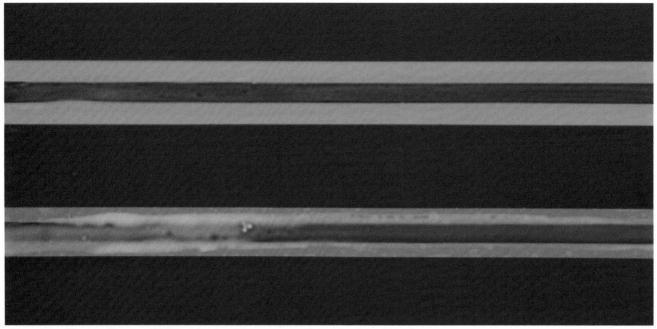

Use either Finesse Tape or 3M Blue Line to make a quarter line stripe in gold leaf.

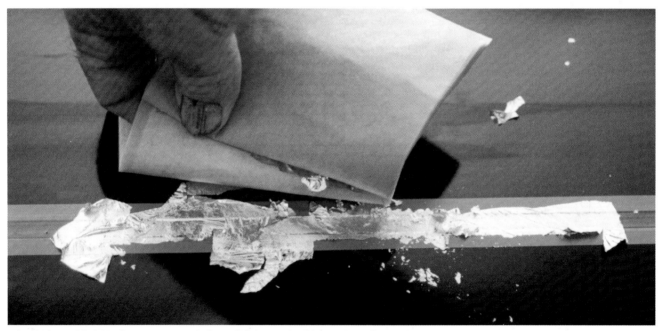

Once the gold sizing is set up enough for guilding, apply either gold leaf or variegated leaf.

Applying Straight Gold or Variegated Gold Leaf

Let's do a quarter line using both Finesse 1/4-inch stripers tape, laying 1/4-inch tape first to establish exactly a 1/4 inch measurement. We then tape both sides with 1/4-inch blue fine line tape.

After filling in the open space with whatever adhesive/gold size you're going to use, follow directions on the can. Drying time will vary from product to product. Always paint a small "test area" somewhere on the same surface away from the work. Use this test area for checking how dry the size is and how well the leaf will stick to it. To see if it's dry enough, use a "tap test." Using the back of your index finger, tap the surface of the gold sizing first to check the dryness. Then run lightly over the surface in the same way. If it seems too tacky, then let it set for a little longer. Next, apply the leaf carefully and in an area that has no wind or drafts. I use a brayer to press down the surface of the leaf once it applied. I bought mine from Speedball. Most arts and crafts stores and sign supply companies sell them. They're also great for pressing down photos on mounting stock. The one shown here is of 1 1/2-inch wide variety. Brayers are also available in 3 1/2-inch widths. You may also use the palm of your hand.

If you're doing variegated gold leaf or real gold leaf (23-karat gold or 12- to 13-karat white gold) then

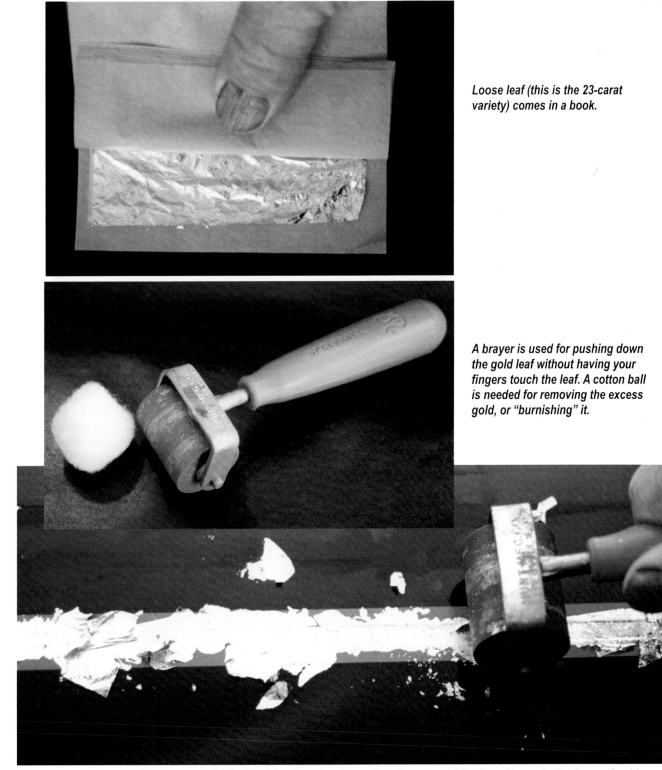

Loose leaf (this is the 23-carat variety) comes in a book.

A brayer is used for pushing down the gold leaf without having your fingers touch the leaf. A cotton ball is needed for removing the excess gold, or "burnishing" it.

Be sure to apply enough pressure to the leaf to drive the edges down into the edges of the tape. If you don't, pieces of gold won't adhere to the sizing.

let everything dry thoroughly. There are two types of real gold leaf. Loose leaf, which is just what the name implies, should only be used indoors. "Patent" leaf, which is lightly bonded to the surface of the paper, can be used in outdoor conditions as well as indoors.

The next step is to "burnish" the leaf. Start lightly rubbing back and forth across the leafed area with a soft cotton ball to remove the excess gold. If you want to try "engine turns," also known as spinning or burling, on the leaf surface, then allow the leaf to almost completely dry before applying the leaf. For engine turning gold leaf, you need a very hard base or the center of the turn will burn out and the sizing will show through. There's no saving a problem like that.

Here are the three types of leaf. Left to right: 23-carat gold, 12-carat white gold (also known as silver leaf), and variegated leaf. This one is red variegated.

Once you have finished guilding, or bonding, the leaf to the sizing, take a cotton ball and remove the excess leaf.

Just clean up the mess and start over if you can.

For engine turning, I recommend using old velvet from a dress or blouse. You can find this stuff at a thrift store. Velvet is very soft and won't burn or tear the gold. Use a small swatch 3 inches square. Simply cover your thumb with it and start to turn the swatch in a clockwise motion about a half a turn each time. With a little practice you'll figure out just the right pressure for your thumb.

There are other methods of turning gold leaf. You can use different size "nurells." These are devices are

A "nurelling" tool is used to make "engine turns" or spins in the gold leaf. You see this effect on a lot on fire trucks and some racecars.

Here is the proper way to engine turn gold leaf. It's important to apply just the right amount of pressure when turning the tool.

generally made of a pencil or dowel with a piece of foam rubber or cotton ball on the end, and velvet covering the foam or cotton. Nurell sizes run from 1/4 inch on up. Bigger sizes will obviously give you bigger turns.

Again, you'll definitely want to practice some engine turning before actually doing it on someone's vehicle. To burnish the engine turn with a nurell, place the nurrell on the surface of the gold and turn it a half a turn, slightly overlapping each previous turn. Wipe or blow off the excess gold leaf around the edges being careful not to touch the engine-turned surface.

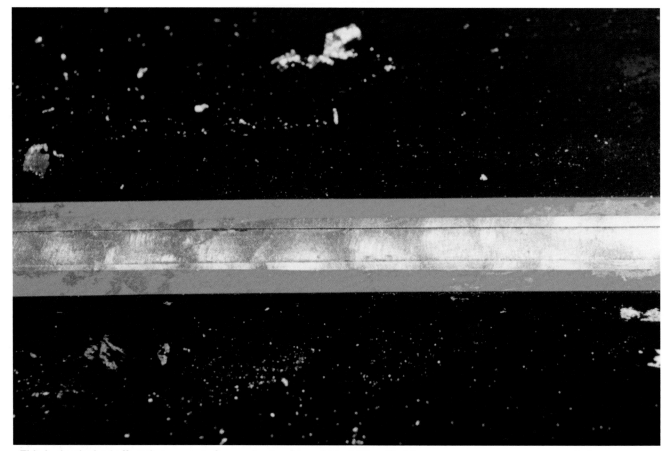

This is the desired effect that you get after engine turning gold leaf. The effect becomes even more pronounced when clearcoat is applied.

Applying Clear

Once all the gold leaf is down and finished, it's time to apply the clear. To begin this process, peel off both sides of the tape next to the line. You want to have a clean edge to cover with the clear. You also want to go slightly over both edges to cover up the sharp edge of the sizing and leaf.

Try to use a an automotive quality urethane clear. All the major automotive paint companies have this product — some are better than others. I've used DuPont and PPG and they work well for me. House of Kolor is particularly good because of its focus on custom paint. I use the product with catalyst added strait out of the can with no reducer added for brushing the clear. If you're

clearing over an entire area, follow the manufacturer's directions. Urethane clear is very expensive. If you can find someone at a body shop to sell you a small quantity of clear and catalyst, I would go in that direction. Unless you're prepared to have a large quantity of clear around, it's kind of a waste of money to buy a lot of it. It's something that you might not use very often.

Marine Spar Varnish is the most reliable clear for this type of work. It lasts much longer than urethane or enamel clears. It also takes a long time to dry and you need two coats.

When all the leaf is down and clear is applied and dry, you can proceed to your outlines.

A Little Band of Gold

Applying a single line of gold leaf in this instance is a little different than taping it off. It can't look as if it's been taped off. For this, you'll need your pounce bag.

Take the pounce bag and lightly tap it over the surface of the area to be striped. Cover everything within 2 inches of the line. After powdering the area, lightly

Take a bag full of "whiting" or baby powder and lay a thin layer of powder on the surface. This will stop the excess leaf from adhering to the surface.

Take an air blower or a can of compressed air and blow off the excess powder from the pounce bag.

Once the line has been clearcoated, outlines can be applied.

blow off the excess powder and leave a light haze of powder on the surface.

To paint in a pinstripe line with gold sizing, I use a quick size during the winter and a slow size during the summer. **Never** do one of these lines outdoors or in the wind. The size will trap dirt and lint and you won't have a good line to guild to. Once the size has set up long enough (don't forget to use a test panel), you're ready to apply the gold or variegated leaf. I recommend using "patent" leaf for this process. Patent leaf is lightly bonded

Load up the sizing in the striping brush and run a line down the surface the same way you would a colored line of paint. Next, carefully apply patent leaf to the surface.

to its protective page and can be used a little at a time by just folding the previous empty page over the leaf area you want to save. By moving the page up a little at a time and exposing just the area you need, you can save a great deal of the leaf. Use your brayer to carefully push down the leaf. Let the line of gold sit overnight if possible to get a good "set." Once the line is set, use a cotton ball or a damp soft rag to wipe off the excess leaf.

You can use a brayer, but I prefer pushing the leaf down on the surface with my finger.

After applying and guilding leaf, remove the excess with a cotton ball, being careful not to get any "holidays" in the edge.

Gold Leafing Fire Engines
with Bob Bond

The practice of using genuine gold leaf to decorate fire engines dates back to the 1800s. Today we find gold leaf all around us — on bank windows, signs and race cars, and on antique fire engines.

There are two types of gold leaf applications. "Water gilding" is when gold is applied to the underside of glass, creating a gold mirror appearance. To achieve texture, glass artisans often sandblast or glue chip the areas to be gilded. The second type of gold leaf application is "surface gilding." With this method, gold can be applied to virtually any type of surface.

Rough surfaces such as rocks, untreated wood, walls, ceilings and statues (like the Statue of Liberty flame) must first be sealed using a shellac, lacquer, sanding sealer or primer of some sort. Since we're primarily concerned with gold leaf on vehicles, we'll concentrate on gilding smooth, pre-painted surfaces.

Gold leaf was the first reflective material to help fire engines stand out. From the beginning, fire engine manufacturers incorporated countless gold flourishes with shading and highlighting effects to separate their models from the competition.

Very few fire departments today use genuine gold leafing on their equipment. The market for this type of work is in restorations of historical fire engines.

The thought of applying gold leaf intimidates some people, but there's really nothing to be afraid of. It's simply a matter of understanding the materials and knowing a few tricks. In a nutshell, gilding is the application of extremely thin sheets of metal leaf. The leaf adheres to the vehicle surface using size.

When applying slow size, make sure that you have a dust-free environment. Any glue that takes 12 to 24 hours to set up can accumulate a lot of debris. I recommend keeping the floor wet while the size is drying. This will help prevent dust particles from being stirred up. The

When beginning a historical fire engine project, start with research. Gather as many photos of similar engines as possible from books, the Internet, newspaper photos etc. Once you have the designs drawn out on paper, perforate holes in the drawing using a pounce wheel. Transfer the drawing into place by rubbing a pounce bag (white powder or chalk wrapped in a piece of material) over the image. When you remove the piece of paper you will see small dots on the surface showing where to paint the glue. This works great when you have to duplicate a design several times. For long lines, blue or green Fine Line tape.

Using 1 Shot's #4008 Quick Dry Gold Size mixed with a small portion of metallic gold powder for visibility, brush on the size (glue) between the pieces of tape on lines and inside the dots on designs. Make sure the size is brushed on smoothly and evenly with no heavy or sagging areas. Start applying the size on the bottom lines/designs and work your way upward. This prevents particles of gold from falling and adhering to sized areas not yet covered in gold. Also, you can reduce the size slightly as needed using 1 Shot's high-temperature reducer #6002. Make sure this part is done in a controlled environment, as dust and particles in the air will show in the gold.

advantage of slow size is that it can dry overnight and give extra brilliance to the gold. The advantage to quick size is the gold can be adhered a lot sooner. 1 Shot has a great new quick size #4008, and it's all I use now.

I always recommend straining the size into a small cup and mixing in a small amount of superfine bronzing powder, which gives a little color to the otherwise transparent size. It just makes everything a little easier to see while you work. I also mix in a very small amount of Smoothie (fisheye remover). Before applying any size, make sure the surface is prepared and all wax and polish is removed.

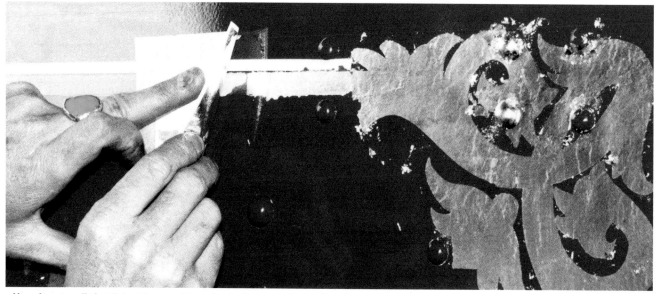

Here it gets a little tricky. You want the size to dry enough to allow the gold to adhere, but not too much that the gold doesn't stick. The drying time can take anywhere from 45 minutes to a couple of hours, depending on the temperature, humidity and environmental conditions. Test the sized area using the back of your knuckle. Touch it very slightly and see if it's almost dry. You want it to have very little tack. When it's time, work quickly. If you don't go as fast putting on the gold as you did painting on the glue, it will set up too much and it will be hard to make the gold stick. Use 23k "patent" gold leaf. This leaf comes on thin sheets of tissue; all you have to do is rub the gold onto the glued area.

To remove the excess gold around the edges, simply rub your finger with very little pressure in small circles over the edges of the gold. If an engine turning effect is desired, place a piece of cotton into a piece of velvet and tape it together at one end, making a spinner pad. Hold the spinner pad against the gold and rotate clockwise about a half a turn. This will put fine scratches into the gold, making light reflect 360 degrees in each circle spin. Overlap each circle spin. On long lines, always keep the center of the circles in the middle and in line with each other in the gold leaf stripe. For the clear, I use 1 Shot's #4006 Super Gloss Tinting Clear and let it dry overnight. Again, this can be reduced using a high-temperature reducer.

Once the area is cleaned, it's ready for application of the size, which can be done by either spraying or brushing. Spraying delivers the smoothest application of size; the hard part is all the masking you would have to do. When brushing on the size, use good-quality gray/brown squirrel-hair sign brushes.

Gold leaf is available in various karats. You can also purchase white gold, silver, copper, aluminum and variegated leaf. All fire engines are done using pure gold leaf. The high-karat pure gold comes in 3 3/8-inch squares. I recommend using patent gold, which comes adhered to sheets of tissue making it simple to apply. Another advantage is that patent gold stays on the sheets and can be recycled. The

For lettering and striping gold outlines, you can use Fine Line tape placed 1/8-inch above and below the gold leaf stripe. Simply paint the black up to the edge of the gold, overlapping slightly, and paint to the tape's edge. Most times I freehand stripe all the black, but taping will work if you aren't skilled at freehand striping and outlining.

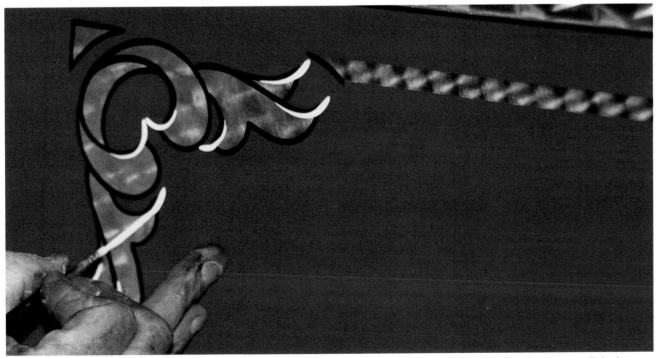

Quite often, historical fire engines received elaborate design work. This was achieved by creating free-flowing scroll designs interconnected with the striping. Each design got special treatments in detailing. You can add highlights, shadows and three-dimensional effects to give the designs more style. Here I'm freehand painting the design detail using an outlining lettering quill brush.

gold comes 25 leafs per book and 20 books (500 leafs) per pack. Naturally, when purchasing gold leaf, the cost per sheet varies according to the quantity purchased. Purchasing by the pack is by far the best deal. I get my leaf from Sepp Leaf Products, Inc., or Esoteric Sign Supplies.

Applying the Gold

Determining when the size is ready is really the hardest part of gilding. If you apply the leaf while the

You can keep the outlining straight and consistent using Fine Line tape. All the Fire Engines in Burbank, California, bear my mark.

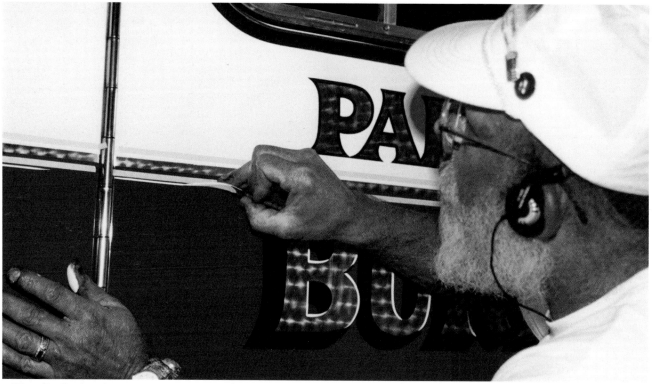

When I'm freehand striping I always place a piece of masking tape next to the gold leaf stripe and hold onto its edge to keep my lines straight and non-wavering.

size is still wet, the leaf will not adhere correctly. If you try to apply the leaf too late, the gold won't stick without a lot of pressure. I test the sized area with the top of my knuckle to avoid any fingerprints with very light pressure. The perfect time for application is just before the size gets

too dry; you want a little bit of tack, but not much.

Since the gold is going to be put onto a vehicle surface, you must clearcoat the gold for protection against rubbing, waxing and washing. Some people use automotive clears, but I prefer 1 Shot's #4006 Super

The city of Burbank shows pride in its fire equipment. Not too fancy, just enough style to be different. Give the gold leafed areas a final coat of clear, wax often and re-clear every couple of years to keep the gold preserved for years to come.

This cool fender ornament design is found on an American LaFrance.

High Gloss Tinting Clear. I apply the clear immediately after putting on the gold. I recommend re-clearcoating every other year over the gold leafed area. Don't use heavy chemicals, high-pressure washers or an abrasive wax on leafed vehicles.

To see more samples of Bob's fire engine gold leafing visit his Web site at www.bobbondart.com.

SPAAMFAA (The Society for the Preservation and Appreciation of Antique Motor Fire Apparatus in America) is a group headquartered in Syracuse,

This corner ornament design was placed on the hose compartment.

This ornament appears on the sides of the seat.

This Model A fire engine was painted for a private collection in Japan.

New York, that is dedicated to preserving old fire engines. For research on antique fire equipment, I recommend *American Fire Engines Since 1900* by Walter McCall and *A Pictorial History of the Fire Engine Vol. 1 and Vol. 2* by Matthew Lee. Some original fire engines contained water-soluble gold leafed decals; these decals can be purchased from Ken Soderbeck's Hand-in-Hand Fire Engine Restoration Co. at (517) 789-6290.

The designs on the fender and hose compartment obviously work together on this 1921 machine.

Striping and gold leaf were used extensively on machines that are antiques today, such as this horse-driven fire wagon.

Chapter Eight

Let's Get Graphic

Eat your heart out Jackson Pollack, it's art on the move! This original design idea came from Steve Kafka.

Back in the 1950s when modern striping first was seen, graphics were unheard of. But today the old ideas like traditional flames, panels, and scallops are still considered graphics. I was still custom painting when graphics first came on the scene. It was a big deal and an overwhelming trend that still continues today completely unabated. Murals, " chaos graphics," tribal flames and "fire" are all modern transformations of the original art of custom automotive painting. However, how it relates to striping is a little different. The obvious answer is outlining the graphics once they are painted. The not-so-obvious is how we as pinstripers can do our own custom painting using enamels like 1 Shot to apply many of the custom paint effects done in urethane enamels and buried under clear.

When I quit custom painting I thought I would never have to learn the art of graphics and how to design them and lay them out. " Wrongo de chongo"! Graphics came around in the mid to late 1980s. You have to develop your design talent to be able to do graphics well. It's like anything you have to learn. It takes time and you must be patient with yourself. Having a good "morgue file" of ideas is a huge help. Depending on what you're specializing in as a striper, you will adapt to the art and start to create your own look in due time. One of my favorite ways to describe the art form is "how many ways can you spell graphics." The designs are endless. Whether you use pre-cut masks using designs someone else already came up for your convenience or you design and lay out your own work, you will never be at a loss for new ideas. Since the subject of design in graphics is so vast, I will only have room to discuss the way the custom effects are done and how they can relate to each other in a full layout on a vehicle.

Thumbnail Sketches

If you're really interested in getting something done in a relatively short amount of time, always plan ahead. Whether it's just plain laying out the design or using a thumbnail sketch, use your God-given artistic talents and put something down before starting on a graphic job. I have a video camera with still shot capabilities and I use it quite often. I'll get a shot of the vehicle that I'm going to do and print the picture out 8 X 10 inch, then make copies of it from a copier. I'll shoot 3/4 front and back and a full side — whatever it takes to get a good shot of the subject — then start drawing out my sketches of graphics on the copies. A digital camera will work, and so will actual prints of the pictures. Just blow up the picture to a letter-size piece of paper in the copier.

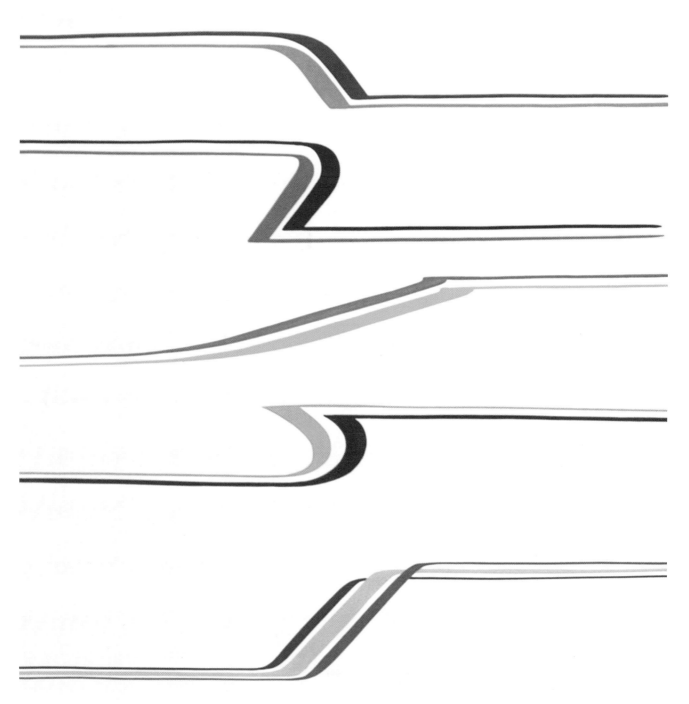

These thick-and-thin graphics start from two pinstripe lines, become graphics, then end as pinstripes.

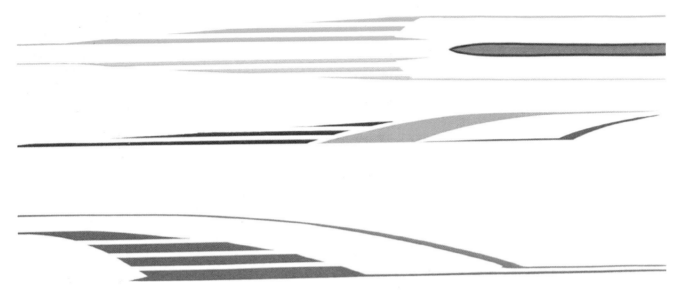

These graphics were done by Bob Iverson.

No copier? Use a projector. If you know how to use a computer, you can even get the proper scaling of the vehicle and apply your graphic to it from clip art.

You don't need a lot of special equipment to do graphics either at your shop, garage, or onsite. If you accumulated all the stuff I mention in Chapter 2's "Let's Go Shopping" section, you're all set. I'll go through each effect and show you a list of things you need to pull each one off.

Sponging and Blending Colors

We discussed sponges in the previous chapter on flames, but there are other sources of sponging, namely the Ocelo or kitchen sponge. The foam rubber sponge produces very fine dots that completely fill painted areas. The Ocelo sponge is a brand name. It's also referred to as a cellulose or kitchen sponge. It has a very nice "Swiss cheese" sort of look to it. I use the cellulose sponge when I want a special effect inside a quarter line or larger. The sea sponge leaves a very large and uneven dot pattern. I've found this sponge great for trailing dots off in a graphic that looks like it's breaking off from itself.

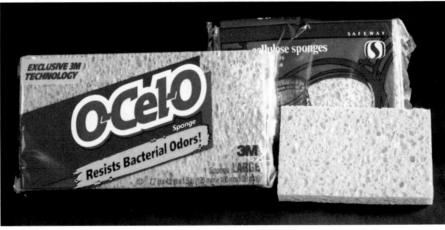

Ocelo, or cellulose, sponges are great for a medium-sized sponging effects.

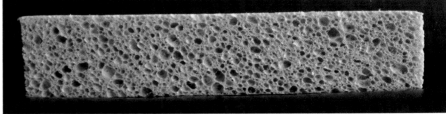

Swish cheese is what this reminds me of. It's a nice look for a 1/4-inch line or other small graphic area.

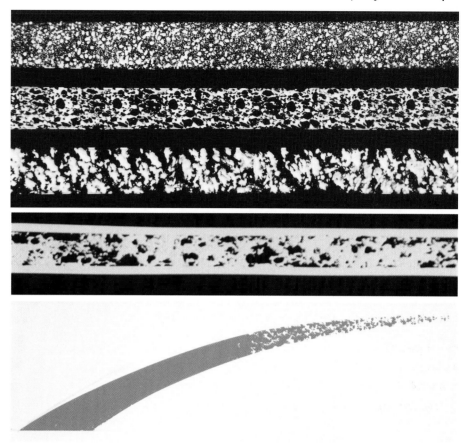

Here we see the three types of sponge effects in one place. Top to bottom: Sponge rubber, cellulose sponge, and sea sponge.

This what a cellulose sponge fill looks like with the same color (gold) for an outline. Very classy.

A sea sponge can be used to produce a trail of dots to simulate a blend from solid to infinity.

Airbrush Highlights, Shades, and Blends

Effects can also be accomplished using an airbrush, but you must sand the base coat first before spraying.

For this stuff, showing the finished product is better than showing each step. It's simple and easy to do once you get the hang of it. Let's take a graphic and see what we can do with it.

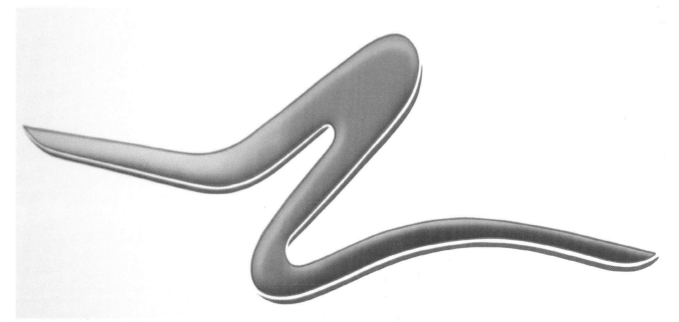

This is the finished blended color graphic with airbrushed highlights and shades outlined and drop shadowed.

Lay the graphic out in tape first or do some sketches and figure out what to do from there. Since we will be spraying the blend it's a good idea to completely mask the area to prevent overspray. In this exercise I'm using transfer tape to mask the area after the masking tape has been applied. Cut out the graphic area with an Xacto knife, remove the tape and press down the edges to prevent overspray. Start spraying the first color. Always

First tape off the graphic with 3M fine line tape. Mash down the edges with a squeegee or your fingernail to prevent the paint from bleeding underneath.

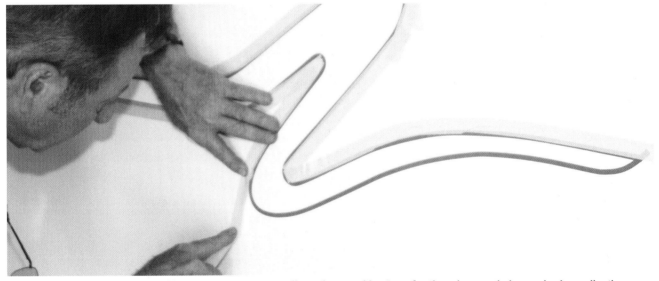

Mask the area around the graphic to prevent overspray. I'm using masking tape for the edges and sign maker's application tape for rest.

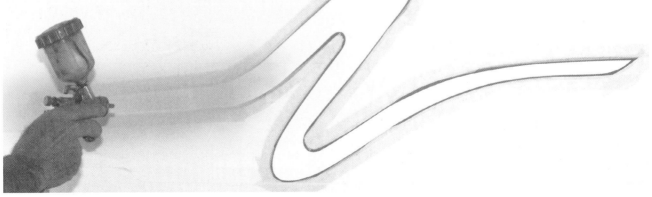

Start spraying the lightest color first.

Spray the middle color and be sure to make the blend even and gradual.

Spray the darkest color last. Again, check to make sure the blend is even and gradual.

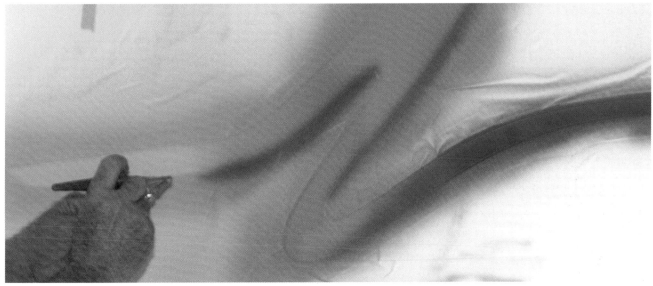

I will use the darkest color of this graphic for shading in my lower edges.

spray the lightest color first and work up to your darkest colors. Spray in the next darkest color, being careful to make your blend even and consistent. You can always come back over with the previous color to even out the blend. Spray in the darkest color of the blend last.

I decided to let the darkest color of the graphic also be my shading color for the graphic. I'm bringing in my lightest color for the highlighted areas. Remember to establish where your light source is coming from before you begin your highlights and shades on the

I then bring in the lightest color for my highlights.

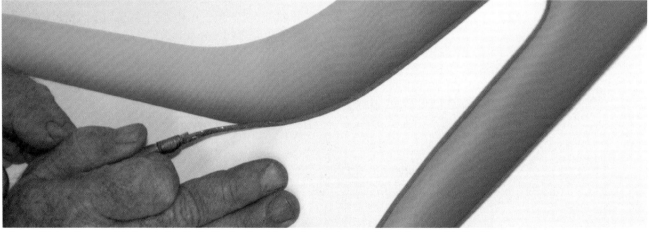

I'm outlining the graphic in a color that will stand out from the background and the graphic itself.

graphic. Outline the graphic in a color that will stand out from the background and the graphic. Don't use too light or heavy an outline. This is one of the details that is the difference between a professional job and an amateur attempt.

The last element I will add is the shadow line under the graphic. If this same graphic was being done on a

car, you could add the year of the car or a name behind the graphic for added flair.

Whenever you're doing graphics like this, it's a good idea to rough up the surface with a piece of sandpaper or, better yet, a Scotchbrite pad. Even if you use a very light-grit ScotchBrite pad, it will still leave sanding scratches and it won't look very good. It will dull the

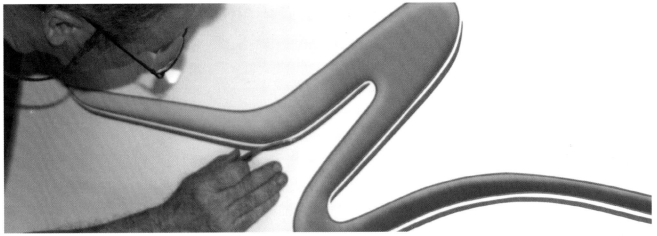

The last element added is the drop shadow line underneath and slightly separate from the graphic.

surface and leave scratches under the paint. Using a solid color coat can help fill those scratches and even out the base of the graphic itself.

When blending with an airbrush, always put down a base coat of paint first and then blend "wet on wet." This will keep the finish coat glossy. I also use a little Penetrol in my 1 Shot airbrush paint to keep the paint coat "wetter longer." This approach allows the paint to dry slower, thus letting the colors blend better. Be careful not to overload the painted area or the paint will run. By starting with a white base, you can blend the color back to the orange and then red.

Vinyl Mask Project

Let's do another exercise. This one will be using a vinyl mask cut from Gerber Mask 4 mil adhesive vinyl. It is cut on a plotter using computer-generated clip art called Splash Mask. This clip art is available through Vector Art. There are other computer clip art disks available that include everything from graphics to pre-designed flames. The beauty of this medium is the option to resize the clip art. One command from the sign program changes it from tiny to full sized. So-called "tear away graphics" use these masks to get the complicated multi-angled ripping effect. We are using a late model Ford pickup to demonstrate on.

Start with your pre-cut mask and tape it in place.

Cut away any mask area that will get into any obstructions. Be careful not to cut away any part of the mask containing the actual graphic.

Start with the pre-cut mask and place it on the vehicle. Most of this mask is made of straight lines. The mask area is more complicated artwork. When you are about ready to apply the mask, make sure all obstructions are duly noted and areas of the mask that are not needed are cut away. When doing the final application of the mask, make sure to have enough help. Long masks can pose problems if you don't lay them down correctly.

To lay down the mask, carefully peel off the paper backing. Longer masks will require two people to apply properly. Don't try to be a hero and do it by yourself.

Using a 3M squeegee, apply your mask. Make sure your mask is squeegeed down into the door edges and the rear of the cab.

Apply the mask with a professional vinyl application squeegee only. Anything else, like a Bond-o squeegee, will not work well enough for the adhesive on the mask to bond properly.

The trick is to get the paint application areas in the proper sequence. Areas that will be masked over, or large sponge painted areas, should be done first. I recommend using different sized tapes to take the guesswork out of laying out complicated graphic stripes. The mask I am using in the example has very specific sizes of straight graphic stripes like 3/8 or 1/2 inch. There are other sizes also in the mask like 1 1/2-inch and 2-inch stripes. Starting from the end of the mask area I lay down my first stripe. It will be 1 inch and it will go all the way around to the opposite side. Next, apply the size tape needed to match the masks separating the area between the stripes. My example has a 3/8-inch margin between the two. These odd-

Now you can start to pull out some of the pre-cut graphic tape, exposing the area to be painted first. Don't forget to plan the proper sequence of application for the colors and effects.

Here are five various-sized rolls of tape. Tape comes in many sizes.

Using a proper-sized tape I am laying down the inside of my first stripe.

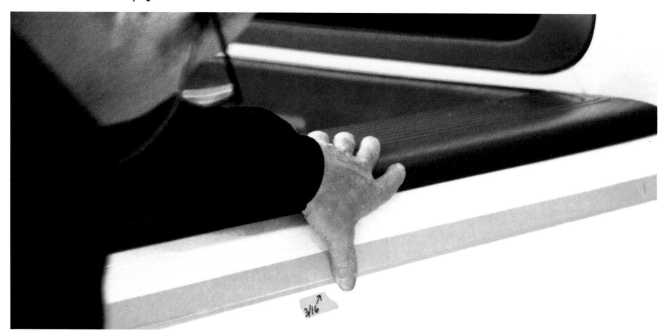

Next, I lay down the tape that will separate one stripe from the other.

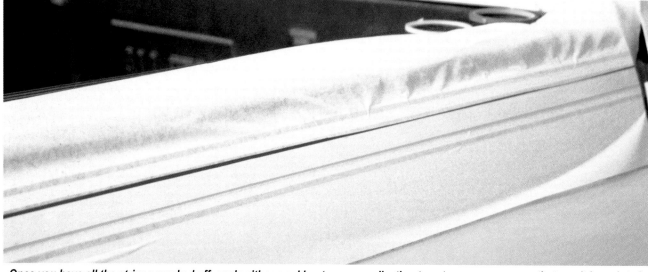

Once you have all the stripes masked off, apply either masking tape or application tape to cover any areas that won't be painted.

sized tape sizes are available from 3M and are included in the #218 green fine line series. Sizes are 1/16, 1/8 and 3/32 inch. This green tape is not for use on sharp corners as it will "pucker" or wrinkle on the inside edge of a corner. For this example project, it's perfect.

Next, we'll mask off the areas that won't get painted. The front fenders get the same treatment. The stripes on the fender will be 1/4 inch and 1/6 inch. I will tape off the 1/4-inch line and hand stripe the 1/6-inch line afterward. I use vertical lines of

Here I'm showing both the 1/4-inch line of tape that needs to be masked on both edges and the tape I'm using to measure my distance on the other fender from the edge of the fender to the line of tape.

Take the tape from one side to the other and measure off the distance to the stripe and lay down the 1/4-inch tape in the proper place.

Tape off the edges with fine line tape.

tape to measure off the length between the edge of the fender down to where the tape should be placed.

Once the other 1/4-inch line has been laid, mask off the stripe. After laying down all your blue fine line tape, don't forget to push down the edges with either your fingernail or a vinyl tape application squeegee.

Granite Effects

One of the many faux paint effects used today is granite or marble. In this example we'll look at how to do granite.

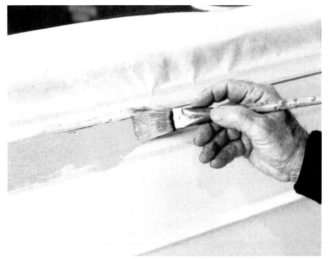

This is the first step of the granite effect. Begin by painting in the light gray.

First, paint the stripe with light gray using a wide lettering brush. I'm using a 1-inch flat brush available from the Mack Brush Company.

The effect of granite is achieved by using Saran Wrap or, for larger areas, clear plastic shipping wrap. Both have the same effect. I will use three shades of grey. Mix up your colors in Dixie cups and put them aside. When you're ready to use the color, pour it right onto the palette, but only pour enough for a few loads of paint. Start applying the medium gray by dabbing the Saran Wrap onto the palette and then dabbing the paint onto the surface. Be careful to not overload the area with one color.Make the color pattern a random sequence, as it would be with real granite. Next, following the same

I use Saran Wrap for the application of the other colors over the light gray base.

Start applying the medium gray by dabbing the Saran Wrap onto the palette and then dabbing the paint onto the surface.

Following the same procedure as before, dab in the darker color.

Lastly, dab in the first, light grey color. Work your colors until you are satisfied with the effect.

procedure as before, dab in the darker color. Dab in the first, light gray color. Be sure that the surface looks like granite. You can work your colors all you want until you are satisfied with the effect. Finally, paint in the cracks with a striping brush. They don't have to be perfect lines. In fact, the less perfect they are the better.

Study the effects before you try them. All you need is a picture in your hand or in your head to be able to make this effect work.

Next, I paint in the smaller line graphic. Use an appropriate- sized brush for the area you want to fill. This will keep your brush strokes to a minimum.

Finally paint in the cracks with a striping brush. These lines should look very random. I suggest studying a picture or piece of real granite before actually applying this effect to a vehicle.

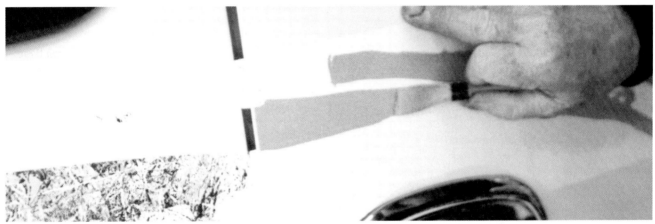

For an airbrushed graphic, use the right-sized brush to apply the color or you'll leave brush marks in the paint.

Once you have the color painted in, start shading the graphic to give it a 3D look. Start with the darker color first.

Once you have the color painted in, start shading the graphic to give it a 3D look. Start with the darker color first. Then apply your highlights. Always keep in mind your light source — this will determine where your highlights and shades will go. Once you're done painting in all your colors, carefully remove the mask and tape.

The outlines around the stripes really make the overall graphic pop. If you don't outline the stripes, the graphic just kind of lays there.

One of the selling points I use when trying to convince a customer to do a job like this is that it will change the whole look of the vehicle. It's like getting something back that's brand new.

Apply your highlights. Always keep in mind your light source.

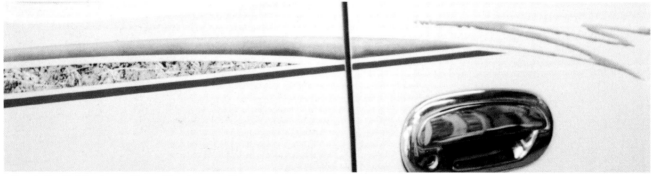

Here's the finished graphics without any outlines.

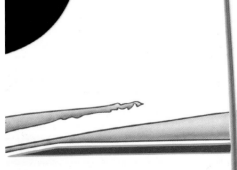

The graphic stands out much better when it's outlined.

This beautiful Ford truck was given a whole new look with a Splash Mask stencil and Vector Art paint. Designs like this can turn a plain white truck into something unique.

Splatter And Spatter Effects

I remember not so long ago that if you threw paint at a car you would be arrested. Not anymore. Now you can get paid to throw paint at a car and the customer will love it. Don't be skimpy with the tape, masking paper and drop cloth plastic on these types of projects. When doing splatter paint, I have found that completely covering up most of the vehicle, especially where the paint will be flung, is an absolutely necessity. Otherwise, you will likely have a mess on your hands afterwards. Believe me, the paint flies everywhere.

You can also use a "texture roller" to simulate the splatter effect. It doesn't look as good as the real thing, but it's a lot easier to control and to clean up afterwards. In addition to "splatter," there is "spatter." This looks like tiny dots of color and adds to the freeform effect of the splatter. To get the spatter effect, use the same hairbrush you would use for the splatter. For finer splatter-spatter effects, use plastic fork for splatter and a tooth brush for spatter.

Here's how I did a splatter effect job on a 1955 Chevy Cameo pickup.

To get the spatter effect use the same hairbrush you will use for the splatter. For finer splatter-spatter effect, use a plastic fork for splatter and a toothbrush for spatter.

A textured roller is used for putting texture in new plaster on walls. It also works well for simulating splatter paint effects.

As with flames, get your graphic layout done in tape first. Once it meets everyone's liking, tape up a piece of 3M white masking paper (like we did in the flames chapter) and start penciling out the lines of the graphic by using the inside edge of the tape. Be sure to use indexing marks at the door edges and the wheel well. As with the flames, once you have traced your pattern, remove it, pounce the holes in it, and move it in to place bare side of the vehicle. Take your bag of marker chalk and pounce the pattern until all the holes have been covered. Carefully blow off the excess chalk with a light stream of air from a blower. Now you are ready to tape up the mirror image of the other sides graphics.

To begin, tape off one side of the vehicle's graphic layout.

Once you have the layout approved, use 3M white masking paper to copy the graphics to the other side. Use a pencil to mark the inside lines of the graphic.

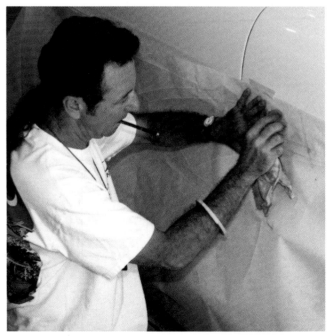

Once you have the pattern in place, tape it to the surface and pounce the holes in the pattern with a chalk bag.

I completely cover the vehicle with either tape, masking paper, or masking plastic. These rolls of plastic are available in various widths from your home improvement store or paint dealer. A word of caution about throwing paint from a hair brush: Be sure to let some of the paint run out back into the cup before you start to throw it on the surface. Take at least one swing of the brush each time you refill towards an area that won't be part of the graphic. It takes a bit practice to get used to throwing paint at a vehicle, but once you get the hang of it, that's when the fun begins.

Once you've gotten all of the first color on the vehicle, start with the second and then proceed to the third. You can do one or two colors, but I recommend using three. The choice of colors is up to you. Once you're done applying the colors, remove all the masking and tape and outline all the edges with a 1/8-inch line.

When you finish applying the tape for your graphic, mask the entire area to be splattered with paper or plastic sheet masking.

Here's the end result: a nice graphic without a lot of trouble.

I did this 1964 Chevelle with bodylines in the front and graphics on the quarter panel. The graphics were done in solid colors, sponge and splatter.

I did this combination of sponge, solid colors and splatter with pinstriping designs for Liz Kitzul of Manitoba, Canada.

This 1964 Chevelle above is an example of using a combination of sponge and splatter, with the sponge work in the checkers gradually fading off and the splatter effect over the top. The front of the panel has solid-colored "hockey sticks" and a trail of sponge in the middle graphic.

The Model T roadster in the accompanying photo came all the way from Canada to my shop for work. I did it in dark magenta, Kansas City teal, and violet. The teal graphic was done in solid color and airbrushed with highlights and shades. The graphic in the front was an outlined splatter effect, and the violet panel graphic behind the teal was done in sponge and faded off on the ends. All the colors were used for the accent striping. The car was done for "Hot Rod Liz" Kitzul of Winnipeg, Canada.

Brushed-on Graphics

If a brushed-on graphic is treated with Penetrol in the mix, you probably won't see any brush strokes. If done right, this way of painting graphics can look dynamite and is only about one-third the cost of painted graphics that are buried under clear. Most brushed-on graphics are in some way airbrushed or have other effects added to them.

Graphic Lines From Pinstripe Bodylines

Graphics coming from small bodylines can add a nice accent to other wise dull embellishments. Any type of graphics requires very meticulous line work. Arches have to be done well and parallel lines have to be exact or the whole thing doesn't work. Bad detail makes the work look cheap and very unprofessional. It's been my experience that if you take one graphic layout, like a five-line parallel that's perfectly straight,

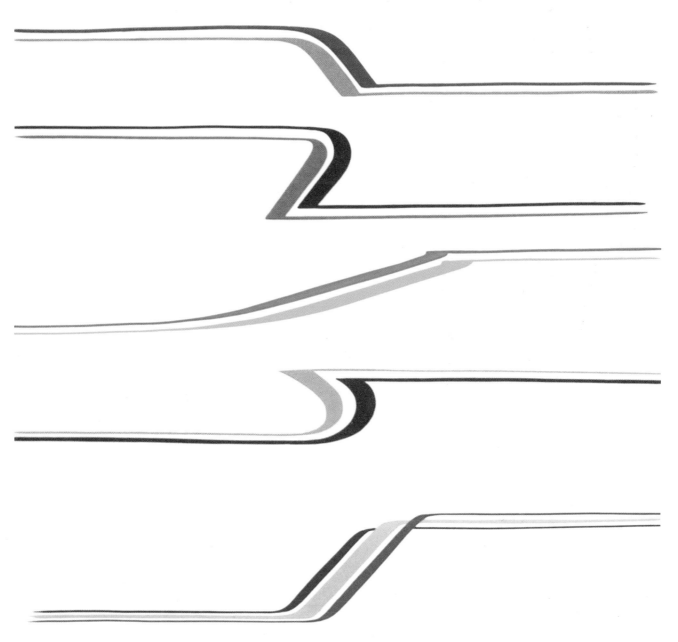

Graphics coming from small bodylines can add a nice accent to an otherwise dull embellishment.

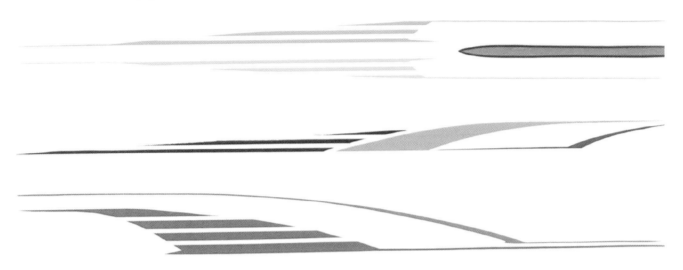

and put a dry brush graphic or a wiggly thick-and-thin worm graphic over the parallel lines, it works. If the parallel lines aren't perfectly aligned to each other, the graphic looks sloppy.

I always use measured tapes for my layouts (1/8, 1/4, 1/2 inch, etc.). 3M, American or Inter Brands (from Germany) all have these different sizes. Outside the U.S. and U.K., look for the sizes in millimeters.

Thin-to-Thick Project

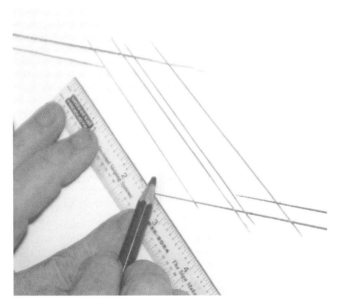

Do a thumbnail sketch in Stabillo pencil first to show where you're going with the graphic.

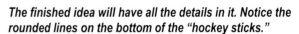

The finished idea will have all the details in it. Notice the rounded lines on the bottom of the "hockey sticks."

Let's tackle a thin-to-thick line graphic. The design possiilities of this sort of graphic are endless and inexpensive. You should add 20 to 30 percent to the bill of a straight line job if you are doing this for a customer — more if it gets complicated.

The straight bodyline can be a little boring without something to break it up. This is what thick-thin graphics

are all about. You can come out of a bodyline, break into a little graphic and back into the bodyline again.

Start by doing your thumbnail sketch in Stabillo. This will allow you to just do the graphic from the bodyline and not have to worry about how big it is if you are doing it right the first time. Do all that ahead of time. Another way of doing the graphic is the exact

Here's the same hockey sticks, but at a reverse angle.

Notice the rounded corner on the bottom of the graphic. This is much better than a sharp corner.

opposite angle. The corners on this example are a little more rounded at the bottom.

All this was done with a quill brush for the graphics. You can fill the wider line areas in faster and with less brush strokes by using a quill brush. The rest is done with a striping brush. Try working with both types of brushes. I've used both to get the job done.

You can also do graphics using tape. The style I'm showing here I learned from watching Bob Iverson's work. Bob's shop is in Huntington Beach, California, and in the middle of the cutting-edge hotbed of automotive art, construction and design. Bob's style eventually lead

him to form a partnership with Bob Bond, and together they formulated the clip art for "Splashmask." Different-sized fine line tapes are used with this style. There are no pre-cut masks. You design your own.

This graphic bases off a 1/4-inch line of tape.

You can start by masking the margin between the upper and lower lines of the graphic with fine line 3M tape and 1/8-inch paper tape. The paper tape is used as a guide and is pulled off before painting.

Notice the angled fine line tape on the left. This is the "angle line "of the graphic. You can make the angle anywhere between 10 to 30 percent, depending on how you want the angle to look. Always mash down the edges of the tape before painting.

I have been a big fan of Bob's work. The first graphic starts out based off a 1/4-inch line of tape. This particular graphic works off of a large margin between the upper and lower graphic lines. Start masking the graphic lines with 1/8-inch fine line tape. Use regular

1/8-inch paper tape for the proper-size separations between the graphic lines of fine line tape. The line of tape to the left of the graphic is masking off the angle line. It's very gradual and because of the very delicate detail needs to be exact in every way.

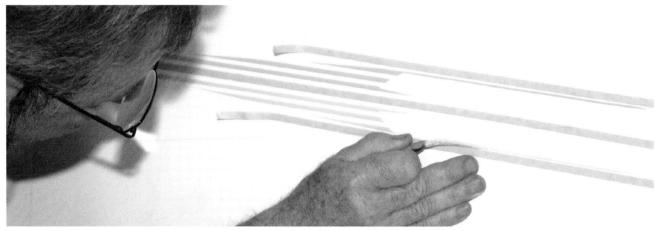

For this example I'm using light blue and green for the graphics and painting in the fine line to finish it off. The last thing step is finishing off the 1/4-inch line in the center of the graphic and outlining it.

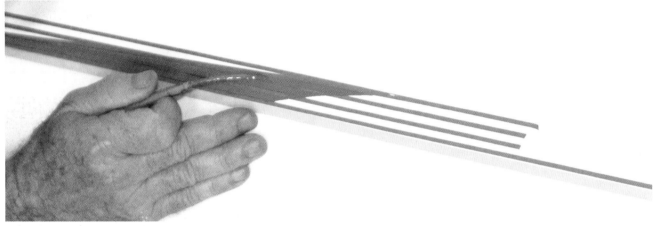

"Cut in" a 45-degree angle at the back of the graphic and fill in the area to the front.

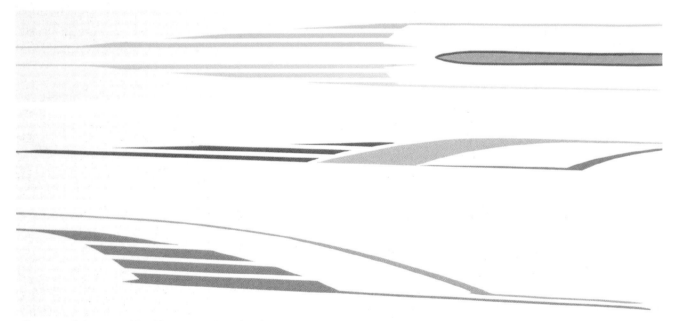

Here are all three graphics. You can see how this thick-and-thin graphic style works. The variety of designs is endless.

Once the paint has filled in the masked areas the graphic begins to take shape.

The three graphics above show how this thick-and-thin graphic style works.

Dry Brush

This is a graphic effect that I would have never guessed would have ever surfaced, let alone be popular with so many people. I saw the effect for the first time at a Rat Fink reunion in 1987. Steve Stanford, the famous illustrator, was showing off his photo album to a few people. Yes, he too started out doing striping and signs. He showed us this new thing he came up with called "dry brush." It was used as an accent, like you would a feather or a teardrop, in various places on a crew cab pickup and a drag boat. I took one look at this and said "if we can make this popular, we can do anything after that." Sure enough, within six months every major car magazine on earth either had the effect on a vehicle on its cover or within its pages. It became huge. Every customer of mine while I was on U.S. tour and on the West Coast in the summer of 1988 wanted dry brush in one form or another.

When I hit the road in 1989, my first stop in June was the Nats East in York, Pennsylvania. I met and became friends with a striper from Phoenix named Steve Kafka. He's the same guy that now owns the Kafka Brush Company. He was doing a dry brush effect called "War Paint." It was bright, it was showy, and it was quick to do — a real moneymaker. And a lot of people wanted it. So I went back home and created my own war paint called "California Camouflage." It was the same technique with a different name. Since I learned this technique, I must have done at least 50 jobs with the whole dry brush thing and hundreds with dry brush included somewhere in the striping and graphics of the vehicle.

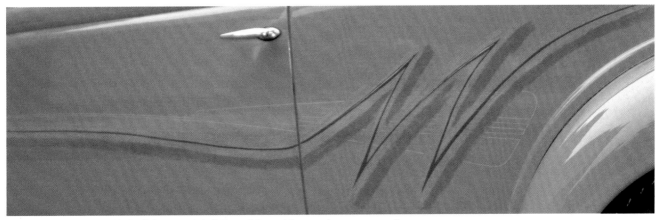

The dry brush graphic look is one style I thought would never become popular.

Thanks to all the major magazines publishing pictures of this trend, this technique made its way to the forefront of hot rodding style.

For small areas of dry brush, you can use a #6-8 brown squirrel hair lettering quill. For a larger area I'll use a 1-inch truck painter's flat lettering brush to achieve the effect I want. First, do a thumbnail sketch in Stabillo pencil to give yourself a plan. This picture shows the real drawing of the graphic. I generally use a single line to guide me while brushing the initial color. Load the brush with 1 Shot paint and use it very lightly on the surface. For my example I will use process blue and pale blue for the shadow.

First draw your layout with Stabillo pencil. It should have a very bouncy, wavey motion.

Load the brush with 1 Shot paint and use it very lightly on the surface to achieve the dry brush look.

The brush stroke should look like this if done correctly.

Paint the drop shadow to the bottom and right of the graphic.

Use a Mack #3 striping brush to do the thick, solid line down the middle of the primary graphic.

Paint the drop shadow to the bottom and right of the graphic. Next, grab a #3 striping brush and load it up for the solid line that goes through the middle of the first dry brush graphic. This line gives the impression of a solid object going through a not-so-solid wide line and brings out the look of the dry brush graphic. I'm using a back-and-forth wave to further accent the movement.

The next step is optional. Some customers like the splatter effect used in the main part of the graphic. Some don't like it at all. If you're going to splatter the graphic, first load up the mini hairbrush and then, using a throwing motion, shake out the excess paint on the masking paper, drop cloth or separate sheet of butcher paper. If you have too much paint in the brush it will scatter everywhere and make a big mess. Once you have a controllable amount of paint in the hairbrush, flick the brush at the area and get enough on there to get the splatter effect you are after.

Once you have all the splatter desired on your

These are the tools that will make the splatter effect: a paper cup, half full of paint, and a mini hairbrush.

First, throw the excess paint out of the brush, then fling the paint onto the graphic. To get the spatter effect, hold the brush close to the graphic and run your finger over the bristles.

graphic, you'll find that there will be some rather large drops of paint along with the rest of the strings of paint. Instead of letting these drops turn into runs of paint, take a can of compressed air, like the ones used to blow out keyboards, and hit these drops with the air and spread them out a bit. This looks better than a paint run any day. The last step is take a rag with a little enamel reducer on it and wipe off the excess splatter. It's your call how much you want to remove. At this point the work really becomes art. Use your artistic talent to judge what stays and what goes. Common sense also helps.

Use a can of compressed air to blow around any large drops of paint to prevent runs.

Use a rag with a little thinner on it to clean up excess spatter.

Here's your new work of moving art, ready for the street.

This graphic was done in a solid color with dry brush added over it in several other colors.

One other simple, quick dry brush effect uses two colors in a straight stripe, 1 inch tall. Start by taping off a stripe 1 to 1 1/2 inches wide. Press down the edges before paint to seal them from paint bleed. Tape the edge further out with 2-inch tape. In a streaking, dry brush sweep, paint in the blue dry brush on a 45-degree angle. Next, dry brush the orange color in. It is a good idea to use opposite colors as they will show the dry brush technique better than a complimentary color. Finally, apply the outline color. This color could be one of the colors used in the dry brush effect, or some other color.

This simple effect starts with upper and lower 1-inch stripes.

Mask the edge with 2-inch tape and start to dry brush in the first color on a 45-degree angle.

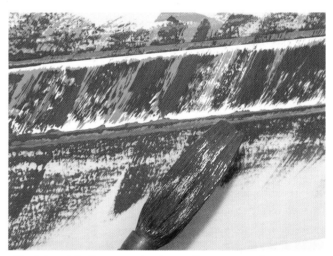

Next, brush in the second color on the same angle.

The last step is to paint in your outline. It can be the same color as the stripe, or another complimentary color.

Saran Wrap Effect

You don't need a custom paint product called "marblizer" to achieve this effect. You simply need a little Saran Wrap, 1 Shot paint in your favorite colors, 1 Shot clear, some pearl powder and some artistic ability. The example here was painted on the hood of my shop car as an experiment to see what I could do with this effect. Always do test panels first before applying the effect on a vehicle.

The marbleized area was taped off in precut Gerber Mask material and then taped off to prevent bleeding through when I sprayed it. Then it was masked up to prevent overspray from getting on the car. The first three colors applied were orange at the top, purple in the middle, and process blue on the bottom. The colors were blended with a small spray gun called a "spot gun." These guns require less paint because their material cups are much smaller than a standard-size spray gun, but still bigger than an airbrush. Once the colors were sprayed the graphic was covered over with Saran Wrap. When covering the paint, wrinkle up the Saran Wrap first. Be careful not to wrinkle it too much or you won't be able to pull it apart from itself.

Lay the wrinkled up Saran Wrap over the freshly painted area and move the plastic around some, then grab one end and lift it off the surface. If you don't like what you see, get some more wet paint on the saran wrap and work it around in the areas that need help until you are satisfied with the results.

Next, grab your spot gun and load it up with 1 Shot Super Gloss Tinting Clear #4006. Do not use their Speed Dry Acrylic Clear #4005. It dries too fast. You will need to thin the clear with either 1 Shot 6001 (low-temp) or 6002 (high-temp) reducer. Follow package directions and safety rules like wearing a mask and spraying in a well-ventilated place. Also, don't forget 1 Shot is enamel and sticks to everything,

The Saran Wrap effect can provide an almost marble-like look to your graphic.

so beware of overspray. Once you have the clear mixed up, add some House of Kolor powdered pearl to the clear for added effect. Alabaster or gold pearl is best for this application. Spray a test panel first to make sure you have the right amount of pearl in the clear. Spray one wet coat over the entire area, being careful to get enough pearl on the job. Next, cover the area with wrinkled plastic and move it around until you are satisfied with the results. You can also pull off the plastic and put it back on for more of a marbled effect, or just put more paint on the plastic and dab it around some to get the desired look.

Chapter Nine

Antique Striping

The Model A Club of America has a very good book available: Model A Ford Paint & Finish Guide. **It covers the paint process, paint colors including striping, and the placement and size of the lines.**

I f you are able to lay lines, you will, at one time or another, be asked to do something antique. Horse-driven carts, sleds and coaches, machinery, toys, scales — it's all been decorated over the years. And, of course, old cars.

If you're not familiar with the way an antique was originally decorated, you're going to be searching for examples of the work. Thank God for the Internet. The Web is the number one way, next to books, to find what you seek. And if you don't find what you are looking for directly, you will be able to find a referral to a book, a magazine, or maybe even a museum that has the information.

Two publications that I found extremely helpful are the book *Model A Ford Paint & Finish Guide* published by the Model A Ford Club of America, and *Antique Auto Body Decoration For The Restorer* by Post Motor Books. The Model A book obviously refers only to the Ford Model A, but has some good information on the paint materials used in striping the original cars and also paint color chips that show the original pinstriping colors used on cars and trucks. There is a section that explains how Ford did its striping, sizes of lines, and paint variation. Another section shows colors, names of colors and where the pinstripes go on the bodies.

Most of the Model A's manufactured in America were striped, and this Model A book is a good one to have on hand if you ever wind up striping a survivor.

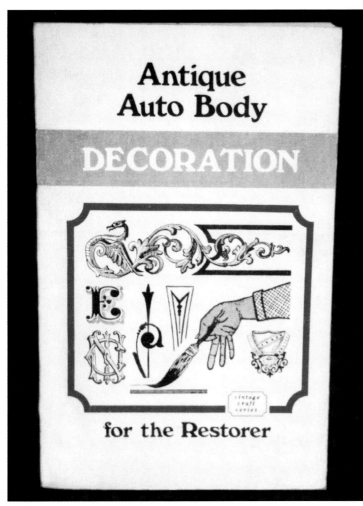

This book is pure gold. It covers all the aspects of antique auto and carriage striping and much more.

I have only seen *Antique Auto Body Decoration For The Restorer* for sale online. This book is pure gold. It describes in detail all facets of antique pinstriping, lettering, monograms, gold leaf designs and pinstriping materials. *The Carriage Monthly Magazine* by Ware Brothers in Philadelphia, 1913-14, would be great to get a look at and perhaps cross-reference today's current brands of materials. The book *The Sword Striping Brush: It's Use & Handling*, and *The Coach Maker's Illustrated Handbook* also provide a lot of answers.

Some of the best information on striping and decorations, including scrolls, monograms, and crests, comes from the vehicle manuals of carriages, etc., that came out before the arrival of the automobile. The craft is the same on both horse-type and horseless vehicles. One of the best sources of research on the decorative arts is the Carriage Museum of America located in Pennsylvania (http://www. carriagemuseumlibrary.org/). The Web site carries much of what has already been discussed here and much more.

If you ever get to work on an antique vehicle, I suggest asking the owner to research the decorations and line designs for you. Often, no one is more acquainted with the subject matter than the proud owner of a restored vehicle. It takes a lot of time and money to bring these things back from the dead, and many restorers will not spare any expense to achieve that goal.

Carriages, Coaches and Wagons

Carriage striping is still around today, although the demand for it is not the same as it was 100 years ago. Major cities such as New York and San Francisco still use these carriages and coaches for special event transportation. New York's Central Park is a Mecca for such "handsome" carriages. They're restored in various places around the East Coast, including the burrows of New York. Others are transported away for restoration in Pennsylvania and even the Midwest.

Around 1994 I asked a striper friend of mine to see if he could dig up some way of photographing a real carriage striper in action. Rob Schroeder of Kobbies Kustom Pinstriping lives right on the Maryland-Pennsylvania border. He sees a lot of Amish folks around and some of them do carriage construction, repairs and restoration.

In his search to find a pinstriper plying the age-old trade amongst these people, he found a young man in his twenties in Stassburg, Pennsylvania, working for his family's carriage building business. There are still stripers around who specialize in antique work, but not a lot of them.

This Amish pinstriper is working on a carriage at a reconstruction business in Pennsyvania. The Amish regularily rebuild these carriages for the transportation market all over the East Coast and Midwest. (Rob "Kobbie" Schroeder photos)

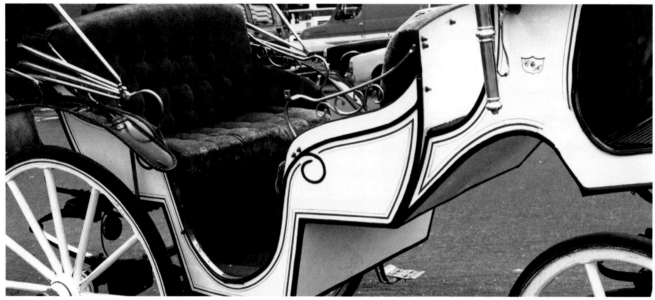

These are simple, box line layouts. Most all the carriages in New York's Central Park are striped in this manner — not too much, just enough.

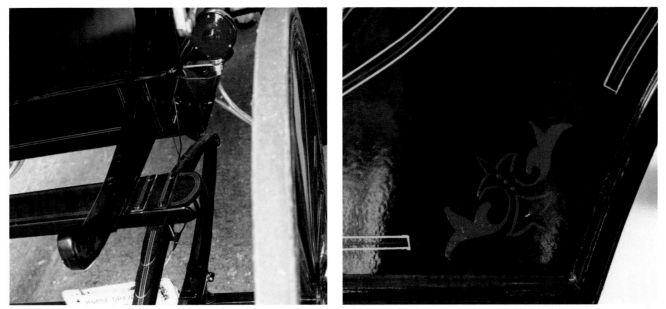

Some of the more elaborate coaches have details like springs, frames, wheels, body corners and large center panels decorated with various forms of filigree and flowers.

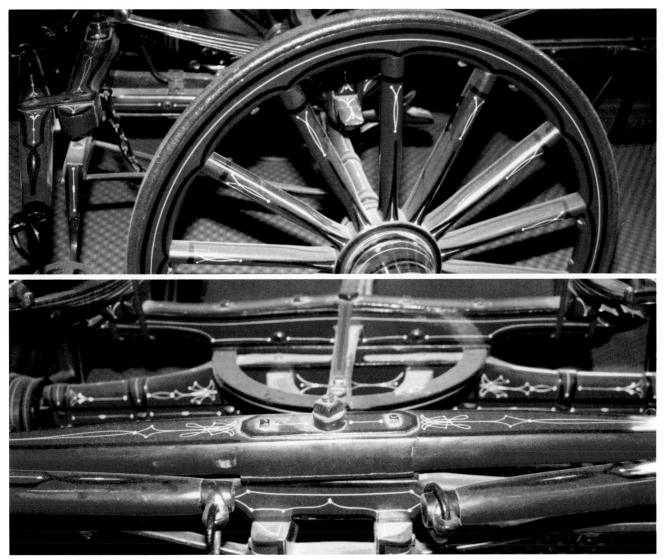

This style is known as "artillery" striping. The wheels also follow the decorative style show here in the framework and spring, frame, and axle areas.

Antique Autos and Horseless Carriages

Many of the earliest American cars were pinstriped at the factory, and the same was true for cars built overseas. The majority of the European automakers striped almost all the panels on their cars. As time went on, less and less striping was added until finally the manufactures stopped striping altogether. However, many of the coach builders kept the practice going.

In the U.S. automakers took a 20-year vacation

This beautifully restored 1933 Plymouth is about to get some wide accent bodylines or stripes. The green 3M 1/4-inch tape is used as a guide for the fine line tape. I use 1/4-inch tape because most of the wider stripes will be at least 1/4 inch or more. Just apply more tape to the layout to make the stripe wider.

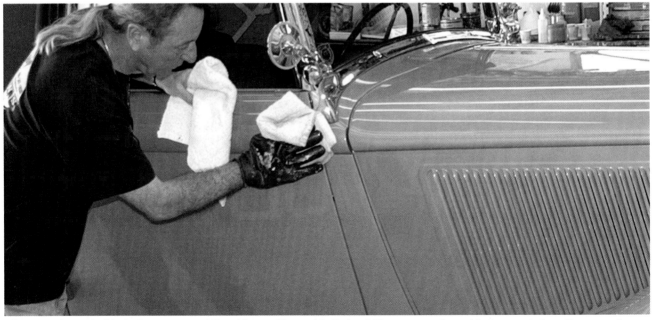

Once you have decided where you want the stripe and how wide it should be, remove the guide tape and clean the area where the stripe will go. You could also clean the area first before applying the guide tape, but if you don't know where the lines will be, how will you know where to clean?

When applying your guide tape, check to see that the stripe will be in line with itself from panel to panel. Panels like the hood and the cowl do not always align well. Make sure the stripe does.

If you're not matching a stripe that was already on the original car, you must establish where the stripe starts and stops. Most times the car's owner will decide this.

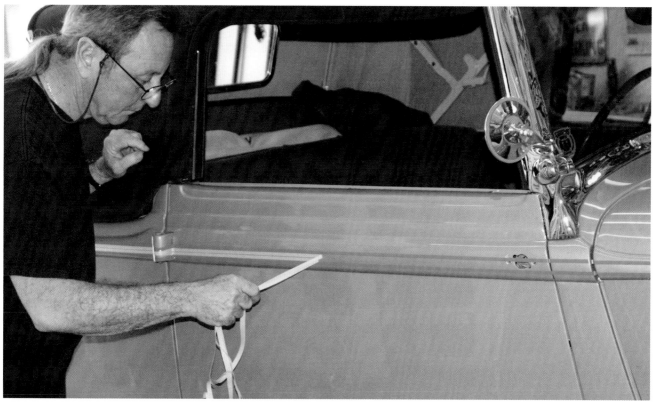

Once you have applied the 1/4-inch fine line tape on each side of the guide tape, remove it, push down all the edges with a vinyl squeegee, and get ready to paint the stripe in the appropriate color. In this example I will fill the stripe area with the color used in the interior and outline the stripe with the dark brown color of the top of the car.

from striping until pinstripes returned in the 1960s. Ford, General Motors, and Chrysler all jumped on the bandwagon, but European cars, with the exception of the most expensive ones, were left without lines.

The striping styles the coach builders and auto manufactures varied greatly. Henry Ford paid his stripers on the assembly line $1 more a day than his regular assembly people. He let them have the freedom

A broad line stripe should be filled in with a broadliner brush. The brush is available from Mack Brush Company.

When filling in a wide stripe, try to do it all in one smooth stroke — almost to the end of that panel's stripe if possible. I always start the line on one end of the panel, bringing the paint as far as the brush will carry the paint load. I then go back over the stripe a second time to smooth out the brush strokes. This also evens the coat of paint out. I then reload and come from the opposite direction, pulling the brush into the line, meeting and crossing over the already painted area. I put a little extra Penetrol into the paint to help it dry slower, allowing the brush strokes to smooth out. Continue the same process with each panel you paint. With the wider areas use a #20 to #26 brown hair quill brush to fill these areas. You will need to work the brush over the wider areas a little more to smooth out the brush stroke.

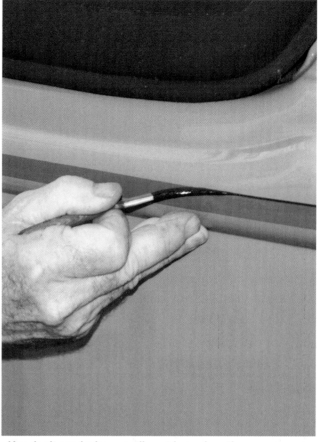

After painting each stripe, try to pull the tape as soon as possible. This will allow the edge of the stripe to smooth out a bit.

You don't need a large outline stripe unless the car owner requests it.

Here's the finished car looking sharp with a brand new stripe.

to do what they wanted and even experiment with wider lines and more elaborate layouts. Rolls Royce put "caning" on its cars. Many a foreign dignitary had his monogram or family crest applied to the front or door of their mode of transportation. Americans did similar things.

The two cars above are both Pierce-Arrows. The bottom example is more detailed, right down to the elaborate louvers.

This 1923 Renault touring car is decked out in 23-karat gold leaf striping. (Nethercutt Collection)

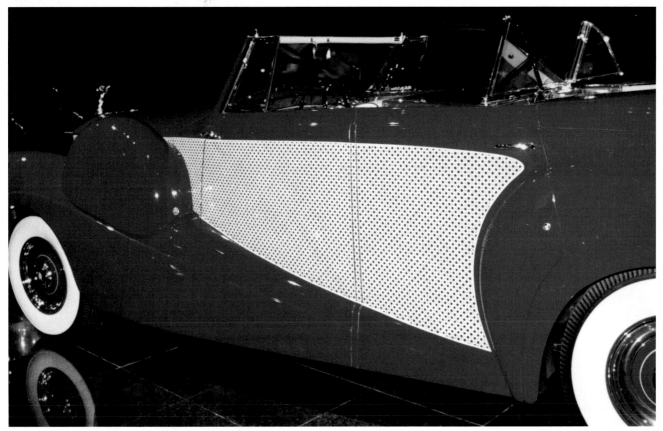

"Caning" came about in the 1920s and was used until the 1950s. The looks of this Rolls Royce are definitely improved by the cane panel.

Level heads prevailed with these two examples of early 20th century auto manufacturing. The 1904 Packard (above) and 1913 Rolls Royce (below) show how understated, simple box like lines can accent the panels of a vehicle.

Many coach builders used this decorative technique to enhance their already magnificent works of automotive art, as displayed on a 1928 Minerva Convertible Town Cabriolet. The effect is simply a matrix done one line at a time. It must have been very time consuming. (Nethercutt Collection)

DEO CONFIDIMUS

Monograms and family crests were very popular among high-society car owners. The crest on top is from a trolley car in London. The initials above are from a 1909 Winton Model 17 Touring. (From the Blackhawk Museum)

Machinery Striping

Antique striping can be found on everything from sewing machines to locomotives. In my travels around the U.S. and the world, I have been fortunate enought to come across some great museum exhibits. Some venues are conducive to photography, some not. Always get permission from the museum if you want to take pictures. Most of what you see here comes from the 1880 World's Fair Machinery Exhibit in the "Castle" at the Smithsonian Institute in Washington, D.C.

Old grinders and presses were often embellished. This style was very popular for breaking up box line striping.

Gold leaf was very popular on larger machines. Notice the use of quarter line striping on the steam-powered engine. The filigree abounds.

Back in those days the tools were dolled up with every form of striping and lettering to impress potential customers. One sign man from Indiana restored the entire exhibit over a period of two years for the Smithsonian.

Motorcycles

Bicycles and motorcycles had a lot of striping years ago. When doing a motorcycle or bicycle for a customer, make sure they give you all the pertinent data on where and how the lines are suppose to go, how thick the lines are suppose to be and the correct colors. There are a lot of examples available from clubs, associations and manufacturers specifically supporting a particular product line.

Harley-Davidson clubs are obviously good places to get information from. The manufacturer is a lot harder to get the facts out of because of so many legalities you must go through to get the information. Copyrights and patents are often very guarded. Early model Harleys, Indians and other brands had a lot of striping and fine lettering on them. Old 1950s model bicycles had a lot on them, too.

Restored Hot Rods

Some of the more famous hot rods from the golden age of hot rodding are now being restored and entered into prestigious concourse auto shows like Pebble Beach each year. These cars deserve our respect because of their importance in the development of custom car building.

One nice thing about striping these cars is there is no room for error. The lines have to be right, there's no guesswork. They have to be exactly like the original car had been striped, complete with the signature of the striper and any other little quirks that were applied to the car. This can require some homework and preparation You need to do detailed photos of every aspect of the striping. At the concourse show level of judging, all the fine details count, and the striper shouldn't be the reason for a car owner losing a show. 〜

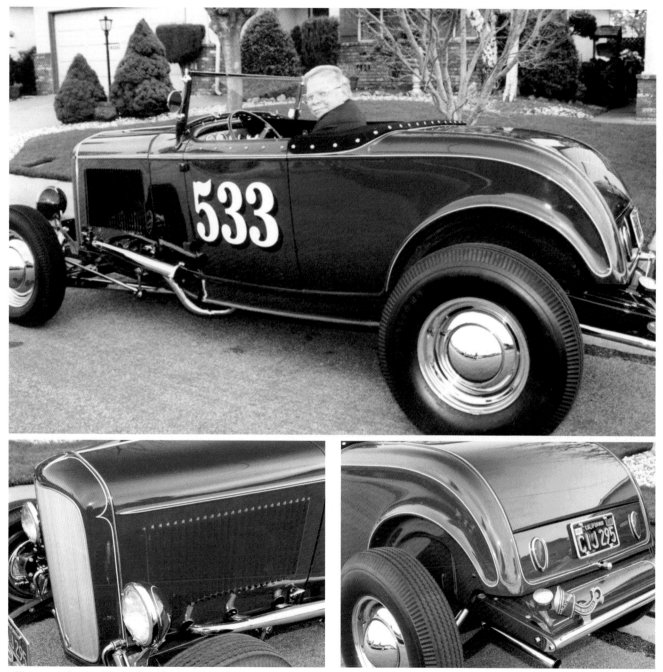

This great hot rod is the Pacific Gunsight Special, a 1932 roadster that was run at Bonneville in the 1952. The striping and signs are simple, but correct for the time. It was shown at Pebble Beach in 1999.

Resources

W e sure have come a long way since the early days of "closed shop" practices and keeping secrets from all our other brothers of the brush. Thanks to the original "letterheads" formed in the 1980s in Denver, the closed-shop mentality went by the wayside. Painters have been getting better ever since. Since the advent of videotape, DVDs, and the Internet, we have been able to archive this vast array of knowledge like never before.

Videos

Next to learning in person with a hands-on approach, video is the best teacher. In video you can see what's going on in movements and then replay it time after time to understand just how the movement works. This is why Eddie Paul and I decided to do our first how-to video in 1983. The video was created in 1/2-inch format to begin with then upgraded the next year to 3/4-inch professional video, re-edited with added shots, and released through Eddie Paul Productions. The next generation came out in 2002 in Circle Scan 4D. This digital-type format drastically increased the clarity of the video. Another video followed with an updated, elongated version for the Eastwood Company in 2004.

In between our productions, there were others who forged some ground of their own in "linear education." There were at least 10 that I know of and maybe more. The company that stands out the most as far as I'm concerned is Mooneyes. They have produced three fine videos in the last 15 years showing all aspects of the craft. Thanks to the efforts of Shige Suganuma, pinstriping, Kustom Kulture art, and good old-fashioned painted signage has flourished in Japan and been kept alive in the U.S. by the Mooneyes Christmas Party held every year in the Los Angeles area.

Others have done their share of teaching on video. Pinskston and Lusk were the next to try producing, followed by The Video Classroom series produced by National Business Media (Sign Business, Auto Graphics, and Installer magazines). Bob Bond's workshop is the main focus of the video's "tool's of the trade" and "brushstroke techniques" segments. *Airbrush Action Magazine* has produced videos on various airbrushing and custom paint subjects. "Kustom Pinstriping Techniques" is one of their series by Craig Frasher, and there is "Basic Pinstriping" by Wizard. Craig Judd has a video and DVD out on the same basic pinstriping subject. Judd's can also comes with an optional pinstriping kit. Overseas is an offering from Kris Johnson of Pinstriping UK. This program is on DVD and only available in PAL format.

The Beugler Corp. has done a few videos demonstrating its pinstriping tool. I would strongly advise purchasing the video if you plan to use the tool.

The Web

Thanks to the "Kool Links" section on the *AutoArt Magazine* Web site, here is an extensive list of helpful Internet sites.

www.vondutchkustomcycles.com
www.fatdaddylines.com
bobbondart.com
www.SATA USA.com
www.beyond6.com
maquinasfantasticas.com
www.automotiveartist.com
www.bakerboyz.net
www.toen-the-line.com
www.reedsigns.com.au
www.siegarts.net
www.noahfineart.com
www.iwata-airbrushes.com
www.artzoneairbrush.dk
www.roadzombies.com
www.weekendtoys.com
www.letterfly.com
www.barris.com
www.hotrodcafe.com
www.pinstripestony.com
www.mousestudios.com
www.comicbookfonts.com
www.pinstriper.com
www.crazyhorsepainting.com/
www.1shot.com
www.vonfranco.com/
www.alcaldecustoms.com
www.herbmartinez.com
www.theletterheads.com
http://www.petzoldts.de/
www.letterhead.com
www.anacondalimo.com/
www.kustomart.com/
www.mackbrush.com
www.geocities.com/ragona
www.glacialgraphics.com
www.moseart.com
www.airbrushsupplies.com
www.eastwoodco.com
airbrush.com
www.doccyber.com
www.bigdealart.com/
slamgraphics.com
www.airheadairbrush.com
www.Acer's Airbrush Art

www.users.argolink.net/vbcoft
Bad Dog Design
www.shadowworksart.com
www.PrimoCustoms.com
www.ronanpaints.com
www.automotivegraffiti.com/
www.dickblick.com/
www.rollingarttv.com
www.daddyodesigns.com
www.mehtola.com
www.airtitefx.com
www.crankart.com
www.graphicsbyfern.com/
www.hotrodart.com
www.airbrushtalk.com
www.fritzart.com/
www.freedomstreetrods.com
www.advancedairbrush.com
www.bartsstripes.net
www.geocities.com/wardgrafix
www.drag-graphics.com
www.semashow.com
www.bikesters.com
www.waykoolart.com/
www.adcook.com
www.visualimagedesigns.com
www.WebRods.com
www.gotpaint.com
www.members.surfeu.de/airbrushpage
www.hothues.dupont.com/
www.zzcustom.com
www.geocities.com/ragona
www.autoartbythekid.com
www.straderstudio.com
www.airdevils.cjb.net
www.shrunkenheads.com
www.airtitefx.com
www.coveredbridgecustoms.com
www.roadsters.com
www.paintwhat.com
www.bobbondart.com
www.geocities.com/mpozar.geo
www.automagiccustoms.com
www.rod-art.com
www.customtruckshop.com

www.wetwilley.com/
www.badgerairbrush.com
www.gasfrompast.com
www.xcaliberart.com
www.hotrodartist.com
www.bikevato.com
www.rccustoms.com
www.motorsport-concepts.com
www.jchetzstudio.com/
www.badasspaint.com
www.photo.starblvd.net/wezover
www.rccustoms.com
www.justhermdesigns.com
www.home.houston.rr.com/ramirezart
www.custompaint.se/
www.brianthebrush.com
www.angelfire.com/ok/airbrushdesigns
www.airbrushpage.de
www.ClassicsAndCustoms.com
www.letterhead.com/articles/bob_burns/
vondutch/index.html
www.beugler.com
www.signspeeweedesigns.com
www.skcscuttingedgedesigns.com
www.custompainting.com
www.brianskustompaint.com
www.letterslinesdesigns.com
www.cosmicairbrush.com
www.geopaint.com
www.muralsbyripper.com/
www.jungledesigns.com
www.ladesigncustom.com
www.airkraftstudios.homestead.com
www.donnowelldesign.com
www.bevart.co.uk/
www.doodlescustomartwork.com
www.hotrodgrafixxx.com
www.streetrodart.com
www.members.tripod.com/WrightBros/
www.crazy-chameleon.com
www.ybarrastudios.com
www.geocities.com/creativedge2002
www.gunpointgraphics.com
www.epindustries.com
www.autopinstripes.com

www.tracksideautobodyairbrush.com
www.dollargraphics.com
www.visualnoisenm.com
tanseycustompaint.com
www.airheadfx.ohgo.com
www.kustomfxcorp.com
www.home.wanadoo.nl/blodshot/
www.aa-gc.com
www.streetrodsofidaho.com
www.customflamepainting.com
www.jimscyclepainting.com
www.cdnratfink.com/
www.thinairgrafx.com
www.handdrawnclassiccars.co.uk
www.sliceofhistory.com
www.fullborekustomchoppers.com
www.speedandterror.com
www.tshirtsunlimited.com/
www.motorsportsillustrated.com
www.baxleydesigns.com
www.universalartwork.com
www.pinstripinguk.com
www.samueldesigns.ca
www.oldschoolflake.com
www.auroragraphics.net/
www.hotpaintart.com
www.manicgrafix.com
www.superfineshine.com
www.be-unique.com
www.theartofvondutch.com/
www.we-bepaintin.com

www.customvehicleart.com
www.holidaygallery.net/thinman
www.daveart.com/
www.webecraftin.com/airbrush
www.graphicsbyfern.com
www.pfeil-design.com
www.cruiserart.com
www.bobbosart.itgo.com
www.b-graphic.com
www.deanskoolkars.com
www.angelfire.com/ab/specialfxautobody
www.deanskoolkars.com
www.martsline.com
www.koolart-usa.com
www.kentbash.com
www.intense-creations.com
www.custompaint.se
www.yosemitesams.com
www.inmotionart.com
www.custompaint.se
www.xoticcolours.com
www.grumpyspaint.com
www.signmastergraphix.com
www.innate.com
www.hotrodpaint.com
www.taylordigital.ca
www.letterhead.com/profiles/tommy/
www.rembrantsbrush.com
www.midevilsteel.com
www.gibbsairbrush.com/
www.pinheadlounge.com

www.spacerods.com
www.rickharrispinstriping.com/
www.tatmanillustration.com
www.woodenclassicwheels.com
www.kustomairworks.com
www.braysonart.com
www.autopinstripes.com
www.v-edge.com
www.paintworldinc.com
www.ivvescustomlack.se
www.rsfsource.com/photo.htm
www.kandmsigns.com
www.geocities.com/pistolpetesigns
www.carrcustompaint.com
www.lowbrow-art.nl/
http://hans.presto.tripod.com
www.stanfordphotographics.com
www.lowbrow-art.nl/
www.3dfoilart.com
www.carizzmacolors.com
www.organicimage.com
www.liquidwizard.net
www.welloiledmachines.com
www.bobsautoart.com
www.automotivebootcamp.com
www.lazerlines.com
www.tlkelly.com
www.pinwheelstripe.com
www.windowjeannie.com

Magazines, Books, Workshops, and Suppliers

The main reason I took on writing this book is because I didn't want to see a book being written as if it were a conglomeration of magazine articles. Books are for spreading out and getting all the facts and figures included in one place. It's a chance to paint a complete portrait of the subject in detail.

But magazines can help tremendously because they are fresh. They are always looking for the new information. The magazine that first started covering pinstriping and pinstripers was a trade publication called *SignCraft*. Since a small segment of the sign trade is pinstriping, these fine folks saw fit to put us pinstripers in the magazine on a regular basis for a while with the "Pinstripers Corner." The magazine is only available by subscription.

Also available only by subscription is *AutoArt* magazine. It follows the trends, techniques and personalities of the custom paint, sign and pinstriping trades. *Auto Graphics* magazine follows the same format. It was the first one out there in 1995 to address the subjects of custom paint field, which includes pinstriping. The magazine stayed around until 1999, went out of print, and *AutoArt* took its place, although *Auto Graphics* came back into print in 2002. *AutoArt* is the brainchild of sign artist, striper, and publisher Bob Bond. Bond got more ink in the 1970s than a printing press. He was always in demand and always willing to work and teach the trade to inquiring minds. He now shares the teaching duties with many writers of the subject of paint and continues to also ply his trade. He now bases out of Lee's Summit, Missouri.

Air Brush Action magazine is covering the whole gamut of information: airbrushing, custom painting, bodywork, pinstriping, and artist profiles are covered. They have a great Web site and a complete line of videos and books.

On the subject of magazines … Over the past 10 or more years that magazines like *Street Rodder, Custom Rodder, Car Craft, Hot Rod,* and *Rod & Custom,* just to name a few, have published special paint and body issues, usually in early spring. Magazines like *AutoArt, Auto Graphics,* and *Air Brush Action* magazines should be considered gold and never be thrown out or abused.

Books on the subject of pinstriping include the recent publication, *Pinstriping Masters* from Nico Press, and *Pinstriping Masters II.* These books are for the intermediate striper and have a collection of technical chapters on all the phases of pinstriping, graphics and cartooning using sign paint or urethane striping enamels. *How To Custom Paint Damn Near Anything* from Motorbooks covers all phases of painting from preparing to primer to pinstriping. *Pinstriping and Vehicle Graphics,* written by John Hanukaine, is another technical book aimed at the basic to intermediate-and-above striper.

Ed "Big Daddy" Roth created some books on pinstriping and designs worth looking at. Wayne Watson has a book out on designs. So does Tramp Warner. Dick Bird has one out, also. All of these titles are available through Sid Moses at Seelig Supply in Santa Monica, California. His Web site is www.moseart. org. *SignCraft* carries many of these books on its Web site: www.signcraft.com.

Workshops and Schools

Most metropolitan areas of the U.S. have trade schools, some of which even teach pinstriping as part of their curriculum of sign making. The best way to get some organized instruction, however, is to inquire about basic pinstriping workshops either through a sign- or paint-related magazine in the classified section (usually in the back pages), or on the Internet. Workshops are sometime two or more days long and require you to go to a location outside of your home turf.

Bob Bond's "Hand's-on Workshops" are held at his shop in Lee's Summit, Missouri. Call 800-BOB-BOND.

The Airbrush Getaway Seminars are held by *Airbrush Art* magazine in various locations throughout the year. Call 800-232-8998. The workshops include a variety of subjects, including pinstriping in a one- or four-day format.

Some professional stripers also hold not-so-publicized workshops in their local areas. Local car shows are good places to find stripers that might teach you. I have people ask me all the time if I do workshops. The answer is yes. Call me at 800-342-1930 or check out my Web site at http://www.herbmartinez.com

Morgue Files

A morgue is for filing ideas for flames, pinstriping designs, or whatever is vital to referencing your work. I've only seen a few guys really get their files in order. Most look like a file folder that's jammed with paper scraps. That's what mine looks like. There are any number of ways of scrapbooking or cataloging your files. The high-tech way is to scan all of them in and save them on disc and in print as well. If you have a digital camera and can set up a copying station, you can shoot all the pictures you want and save them that way.

More Do-It-Yourself Guides for Your Garage Work

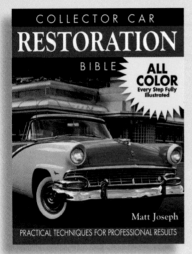

Collector Car Restoration Bible
Practical Techniques for Professional Results
2nd Edition
by Matt Joseph

Approach automobile restoration and repair with confidence based on authoritative instruction and tips for avoiding costly errors. The more than 500 color photos you'll find in this guide demonstrate specific techniques for bodywork, basic engine restoration, and time and money saving tips for creating the car of your dreams; without having to shell out your life savings.

Softcover • 8-1/4 x 10-7/8 • 400 pages
500+ color photos & illus.
Item# AJ02 • $29.99

Eddie Paul's Custom Bodywork Handbook
by Eddie Paul

This customizing how-to introduces and demonstrates many of the latest techniques in more than 200 dynamic color photos. Whether your focus is customizing a classic beauty, rebuilding an old school hot rod or trying your hand at giving life to a modern tuner car, the 20+ projects explained in this book will help you achieve your goals.

Softcover • 8-1/4 x 10-7/8 • 176 pages
200+ color photos
Item# SGCBW • $24.99

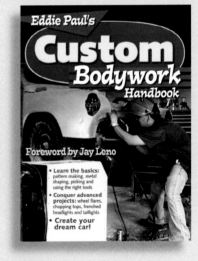

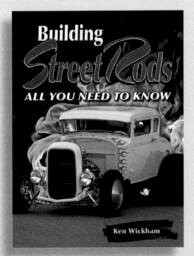

Building Street Rods
All You Need to Know
2nd Edition
by Ken Wickham

Outlines practical tips for customizing hot rods including advice for choosing the right car, handling fiberglass and metal bodies, and preventing paint problems. Plus, you'll find more than 200 stunning color photos that offer a detailed view of the finished product, and demonstrate essential techniques.

Softcover • 8-1/4 x 10-7/8 • 176 pages
200+ color photos
Item# SRCB2 • $24.99

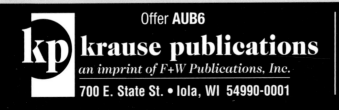